ADVANCE PRAISE FOR

The Preamble as Policy: A Guidebook to Governance and Civic Duty

"In *The Preamble as Policy,* Irons and Twombly find in the Constitution's Preamble an aspirational guide to America's potential, even in times wrought with paralyzing polarization and civil unrest. This is a clever, hopeful book that will challenge readers to think critically about the Constitution, likely in ways they haven't before."

– Joshua J. Dyck, Professor of Political Science,
University of Massachusetts Lowell

"When do you start talking about policy? You start at the beginning. That's what Irons and Twombly have done in *Preamble as Policy*: taking students of government and public policy back to the first words of the Constitution. By anchoring an array of contemporary policy challenges in history and the Constitution, from just policing to welfare reform to anti-trust, the authors invite the reader to critically consider the purpose of government in the United States. They do this in under 100 pages, a feat worthy of a big welcome in every syllabus."

– Heath Brown, Ph.D., Associate Professor of Public Policy, Department of
Public Management and CUNY Graduate Center, John Jay College,
City University of New York

The Preamble as Policy

This book is part of the Peter Lang Media and Communication list.
Every volume is peer reviewed and meets
the highest quality standards for content and production.

PETER LANG
New York • Bern • Berlin
Brussels • Vienna • Oxford • Warsaw

Robert Irons and Jim Twombly

The Preamble as Policy

A Guidebook to Governance and Civic Duty

PETER LANG
New York • Bern • Berlin
Brussels • Vienna • Oxford • Warsaw

Library of Congress Cataloging-in-Publication Control Number: 2021013677

Bibliographic information published by **Die Deutsche Nationalbibliothek**.
Die Deutsche Nationalbibliothek lists this publication in the "Deutsche Nationalbibliografie"; detailed bibliographic data are available on the Internet at http://dnb.d-nb.de/.

ISBN 978-1-4331-8803-9 (hardcover)
ISBN 978-1-4331-8823-7 (paperback)
ISBN 978-1-4331-8804-6 (ebook pdf)
ISBN 978-1-4331-8805-3 (epub)
DOI 10.3726/b18345

80 Broad Street, 5th floor, New York, NY 10004
www.peterlang.com

This work is dedicated to the Founders and Framers of our nation for their words and vision that set us on the path to perfectibility and to the generations who came after them, who by their words and deeds sought to continue that march to perfectibility.

"The purpose of government is to enable the people of a nation to live in safety and happiness. Government exists for the interests of the governed, not for the governors."

Thomas Jefferson

Contents

Acknowledgments

Robert Irons thanks his wife, Ruth Ann for her patience and her effectiveness as a sounding board. Her name belongs right beside his.

Jim Twombly thanks his wife, Denise King for her daily support and counsel. He also thanks Elmira College, particularly the Office of Academic Affairs, for creating an environment that allows for creativity and scholarship.

Chapter One

A Preamble to the Preamble

In 2020, America went through a tremendously stressful period. Much of our public life, both social and economic, was shut down for an extended period due to COVID-19. In the midst of this global pandemic, Americans took to the streets in a variety of protests. There were protests against actions taken by state and local officials to protect the groups most at risk to the virus, some with maskless citizens carrying guns to state capitols (and sometimes into the buildings), fueled by the record high unemployment rates created by the shutdown of all non-essential business. Just as some states were beginning to reopen their economies, four Minneapolis police officers arrested, and in the process murdered, George Floyd over his passing of a counterfeit $20 bill, leading to mass protests in cities big and small, both here and abroad, against continued police violence towards communities of color. A deadly pandemic, widespread unemployment, racial and social unrest, and a government seemingly incapable or unwilling to respond effectively became a perfect storm to highlight and re-examine our founding goals. The current political divisions in this country rival those that were in place just before the Great Depression, with many of the same or similar issues at the root of the division. America is stubborn in learning the lessons of its past, especially if connected to race or class.

As a "perfect" wrap to such a tumultuous year, an incumbent president – Donald Trump – called into question the process and results of the election that led to his ouster. His assertions of widespread fraud and a "stolen election" were aimed at two targets. The first was the outcome of the election, which Trump challenged in both state and federal courts, all the way to the Supreme Court's dismissal of a suit brought by the Attorney General of Texas seeking to throw out the election results in four other states (Wisconsin, Michigan, Pennsylvania, and Georgia), which Trump had carried in 2016. On December 14, 2020, the Electoral College, essentially, put an end to the court challenges by deciding in favor of Trump's opponent – Joe Biden. The second target was the future legitimacy of a Biden Presidency. By exercising constant legal and media challenges to Biden's vote count, Trump sought (if he couldn't win) to delegitimize Biden's Administration.

The "wrap" took a violent and insurrectionist turn on January 6, 2021, when a mob of Trump supporters and conspiracy theory enthusiasts stormed the Capitol during the Congressional certification of the Electoral College vote counts certified and forwarded by the states. The process, mostly a formal and ceremonial one, was interrupted as the mob pushed its way past police officers on its way to the House and Senate Chambers with chants of "Hang Mike Pence" (the Vice president and presiding officer of the Senate) and "Where's Nancy?" (the Speaker of the House, Nancy Pelosi) with later discovered intentions of her assassination. The insurrection was put down or petered out within a few hours and the Congressional certification of the Electoral College continued into the wee hours of the next day. These events were fueled by false claims of a stolen election and a misreading of the Constitution with respect to Congress's ability to do anything other than certify the state-by-state results. Many have argued that such events would have been far less likely in a time that was not framed by hyper-partisanship.

Our Founders and Framers[1] clearly warned us of the dangers of, to use James Madison's words, "the mischiefs of faction." Some have argued that this was a warning about political parties, others have taken it to mean single-interest groups. Entrenched interest groups, with narrowly defined political agendas, have the ears of Congress and are therefore able to influence the passage of legislation in their favor, and in some cases are able to write the legislation themselves. This is most certainly not what the Founders intended.

The Constitution is the foundation of our entire system of government; it spells out what the branches of government are, their relationships to the other branches, what power each branch holds, and how the branches are intended to work together to support and defend the American people. At the same time, it has built-in flexibility in the form of the amendment process; our Framers had the foresight to presuppose unforeseen circumstances. It makes sense that a government formed from change would see the need to anticipate future change.

The Preamble contains the Framers' justification for drafting the Constitution. It explains the need for the document, why it is important to the people of the United States. It lays out, line by line, the motivation for forming the government, and therefore what considerations the people should expect from the newly formed republic. The Preamble outlines the responsibilities the Framers saw as central to the mission of the new government; it is a list of the objectives the Framers felt obliged to provide for the citizens of America. It therefore also serves as a checklist of government policies and their effectiveness at following that original intent.

Our intent with this book is to argue that the Preamble to the Constitution is much more than it appears. It is more than just one sentence, 52 words, offered as the justification for throwing off the yoke of tyranny and forging a new future for all Americans. As Jefferson noted, "The purpose of government is to enable the people of a nation to live

1 When referring to the signers of the Declaration of Independence we will use the term Founders and in reference to those who crafted and signed the Constitution, we will use the term Framers.

in safety and happiness. Government exists for the interests of the governed, not for the governors" (Jefferson 2009, 63).

We intend to show that government policies are effective for most Americans when they are designed to follow the intent of the Framers, as explained in the Preamble of the Constitution. The evolution of the lobbying system in Washington D. C. has resulted in an enormous amount of legislation that is written to benefit specific interests, and is often written by or in conjunction with members of the interests that will benefit. Congress benefits from this in the form of campaign contributions and lobbying jobs after their terms in office are over. Early applications of the "revolving door" hypothesis in political science emphasized administrators. Jeffrey Cohen (1986) nicely summarizes the classic works in this area of research. There is other work, however, that places the revolving door within the body of work known by a number of different names: policy subgovernments, issue networks (Heclo 1978), advocacy coalition frameworks (Sabatier 1986), and iron triangles (Weingast 1981) to name a few.[2] Little if any consideration is given to the needs or wants of the larger community of the American people in this process. Thus, very little of Congress' time and efforts are spent advancing the needs of their constituents – the Framers' list of responsibilities is not part of the equation.

In a republic, the people choose others to represent them and make decisions on their behalf. In other words, a representative democracy. Critics argue, for too long our representatives have been making decisions that promote their own interests, or those of their party, ahead of the interests of their constituents. As voters, we need to hold our representatives accountable for the decisions they make in our service. As citizens of a republic, we have a duty to remind them of their constitutional duties, as laid out in the Preamble, and express our displeasure with their failure to prioritize our needs by voting them out of office.

The Preamble to the Constitution is more than an introduction to this great document; it is a statement by our Framers of what government must do for its citizens. It serves as a guidebook for what our federal

2 Many more examples of the extant literature exist, those listed here serve as exemplars, summaries, or the initial work in the area indicated.

government should be doing for us, so that we can determine for ourselves if our leaders are living up to their commitments. With this book, we intend to show the American people what our Framers thought that they, and their successors, should be doing for us, so that we have a foundation for holding our representatives accountable. In many ways, in writing this book we have been limited in some of the same ways as the Founders and the Framers were. Travel was difficult, nearly impossible during the COVID-19 pandemic and our resources are in many ways thus limited. We, however, have advantages that those working in the late 1700s did not. As they did, so can we use references available in our personal libraries, but we can also access more sources via the Internet and cross the many miles between us, not as Caesar Rodney did by riding through the night while ill to cast a crucial vote allowing the new nation to be born, but by using videoconferencing software.

This is less a work of law or history than it is a civics lesson and a demonstration of how public policy does or does not meet the goals set by the Framers. To be sure, we use law and history to make our arguments. However, we seek more to provide a guidebook for our representatives and a checklist to use for judging the attempts our representatives make to provide those objectives. Thus, it should help our elected officials prioritize what objectives the new government ought to be providing its citizens. At the same time, it can be useful in deciding whom to vote to remain in office and whom to vote out of office.

Approaches to the Constitution

There are many ways to approach the study of the Constitution. One way is through the lens of a "living document" that sees the Constitution as "one that evolves, changes over time, and adapts to new circumstances, without being formally amended" (Strauss 2010). Writing for the University of Chicago Law School's website, David Strauss notes that this terminology is often used by critics with derision. He writes, "the Constitution is supposed to be a rock-solid foundation, the embodiment of our most fundamental principles-that's the whole idea of having a constitution." Certainly, the Constitution needs to provide a solid foundation for our laws and social and political institutions, but it needs to be flexible enough to evolve without constant amendment. This view is often associated with liberal or progressive political viewpoints.

Another approach, generally associated with a more conservative political outlook is that of strict construction or original intent. The law school at Cornell University defines strict constructionism as "interpreting a legal provision (usually a constitutional protection) narrowly. Strict constructionists often look only at the literal meaning of the words in question, or at their historical meaning at the time the law was written."[3] Therefore, a strict constructionist perspective uses the framers' own words and interprets them within the bounds of the common meanings at the time of writing. This is done to apply the legal provision in the contemporary environment, but as it was intended by those who devised the document long ago. Original intent, according to Epstein and Walker (2020), "asks what the framers wanted to do" (23). Original meaning, they note, asks what the words meant to "those who enacted it" (23). Textualism is similar, but focuses not so much on intent as it does on the meaning of the words to reasonable individuals at the time of their writing.[4] To stick to a textualist or originalist interpretation is supposed to mean stripping away political interpretation. While neither of us could ever be described accurately as conservative, this perspective provides a unique tool for examining what the Preamble means. Further, Constitutional scholar Akhil Reed Amar (2005) noted that such forms of interpretation can cut both ways, ideologically speaking. Amar points out that the justice perhaps most well-known as an originalist was Hugo Black, who was "a liberal lion and indeed the driving force behind the Warren Court" (260).[5]

There are a number of other ways to approach Constitutional Interpretation. In addition to the two forms of originalism and textualism,

3 Cornell Law School. "Strict Construction: Definition from Nolo's Plain-English Law Dictionary)," Law.cornell.edu. Accessed June 9, 2020, https://www.law.cornell.edu/wex/strict_construction.

4 Epstein and Walker attribute this definition to Justice Antonin Scalia.

5 It is often the case that Court liberals will employ originalism or textualism when that line of reasoning will achieve their desired outcome and Conservatives on the Court will likewise become adherents to a living document view when it suits their needs.

Epstein and Walker (2020) list structural analysis, *stare decisis* (applying more to decision making by the justices), pragmatism, and polling other jurisdictions (also more applicable to how the justices decide). Structural analysis or structuralism refers to the practice of judging a law's constitutionality in the context of the overall structure of the Constitution and how the law might fit in the larger context of the document. *Stare decisis* is a Latin expression meaning "let the decision stand" and thus refers more to the application of precedent to contemporary interpretation and application in specific cases. It is often noted that adherence to the practice can turn liberals into conservatives and conservatives into liberals. For example, for many years Associate Justice William Rehnquist voiced opposition to the practice of reading suspects their rights as a result of the Court's ruling in *Miranda v. Arizona* (1966), but when faced with the opportunity to vote against it while Chief Justice, Rehnquist demurred. When asked why he changed his mind he cited the precedent and noted that the practice had become so ingrained in our culture that to undo it would cause more harm than its existence. Pragmatism is sometimes thought of as "balancing", contrasting "the probable practical consequences of one interpretation of the Constitution against other interpretations" (Murrill 2018, 13).[6] According to Epstein and Walker (2020), the Court can poll other jurisdictions. That is, look to practices in state courts on similar issues or even to how high courts in other countries might handle a similar question.[7]

Certainly, the best approach to Constitutional Interpretation would at least attempt to establish what the meaning of the words is and make an attempt to derive some understanding of the intentions of the Framers.[8] One cannot willy-nilly apply a contemporary meaning of the

6 Murrill provides an excellent summary of a number of other modes of constitutional interpretation including: historical practices, national ethos, and moral reasoning.

7 Jeffrey Toobin, among others, has noted that both Justices Anthony Kennedy (Toobin 2012) and Stephen Breyer (Toobin 2007, 2012) would often look to constitutional interpretation in other countries as a guide to decision making, especially in cases where domestic precedent was scarce. In the case of Kennedy, this behavior angered his critics from the right, who were already dismayed by his votes with the liberals on cases in involving abortion and LGBTQ rights.

8 In the case of interpreting the amendments it would be the proposers or drafters of the amendment in place of the Framers.

words and be true to the spirit of the document. Meanings of words themselves change all the time and applying the current meaning of a word might be the opposite of what it meant at the time it was originally written. For example, in recent years the word "literally" has come to mean something different from its actual meaning when used in colloquial conversation.[9] It therefore behooves anyone looking at the written use of the word to know that use of it in earlier writing would have a vastly different meaning. That being said, we view the Constitution as a living document that must change with the times and note how often interpretation of the Constitution has changed based on the change in meaning of words. A strict adherence to the words in the document perhaps would not allow for the creation of an air force, but the intent of the Framers to provide for the national defense certainly allows for Congress to adapt to more advanced technology.

The Preamble

What is this thing we've been describing to this point? As many have noted, it is more than just the introduction to the Constitution, it is a statement of goals. It does not have the force or weight of law, but is nonetheless an important guidepost for future policy makers.

> We, the people of the United States, in order to form a more perfect union, establish justice, insure domestic tranquility, provide for the common defense, promote the general welfare, and secure the blessings of liberty to ourselves and our posterity, do ordain and establish this Constitution for the United States of America.

These six specific objectives also serve as examples of what the new republic should be providing the American citizens. They were offered as the justification for rebellion, which implies that their newly formed government would be expected to provide these guarantees. And, we will argue in this book, they also provide a basis for judging

9 More recently, in the summer of 2020, Merriam-Webster's Dictionary has admitted the word "irregardless" into its online version. It defines it as a "nonstandard" usage, but the equivalent of its logical opposite: "regardless."

the performance of our elected officials, helping us to determine which of them are truly working to achieve those six objectives, and which should be shown the door.

While it is clear that the Preamble carries no legal authority, it is also clear that it serves as more than an introductory sentence. Those six objectives are important enough to list as the reasons for creating and implementing the Constitution, which makes them important enough to be used as objectives for our representatives to achieve and improve upon. It also makes them useful for reviewing the performance of our representatives in preparation for Election Day.

They do not carry the weight of law, but they serve as goals to pursue in the decision-making processes of government – they are "ends to be served by the constituted government" (Adler & Gorman, 78). The Framers thought these objectives important enough to use them to rationalize their new experiment in government, therefore our representatives in government should include these objectives in their decision-making process. Their decisions should be intended to maximize the objective in question, to achieve the best outcome for as many people as possible.

These six objectives or guarantees, and the methods through which they are achieved, stand as a playbook for making decisions on behalf of the American public. Essentially, the Preamble serves as public policy. The framers included a short list of the important items the new United States government should use in the creation and implementation of the laws they write, the policies they enact and the services they offer their constituents. In doing so, they also left the American public that same list to use as a scorecard when voting for their elected representatives.

We, the People of the United States, Do Ordain and Establish This Constitution for the United States of America

Part of the purpose of the Preamble is to declare that the Constitution that follows carries the full weight and authority of the people of the

United States, and that the people agree to establish it as our system of government. It is a clear and declarative statement that Americans will govern themselves.

It is important to understand that the act of granting authority to representatives does not abdicate the power to those representatives. The ultimate power and authority always rests with the voting public and is bestowed temporarily with each election. In this way, the nature of the representative government can change along with the nature of the population it represents. In a country formed and fed by immigrants, this crucial property makes it possible, at least in theory, for the government to reasonably reflect the changing face of its constituency.

The struggle to recognize the people as the source of power is documented in detail by Adler and Gorman (1975). They note that the original phrases "we, the people" and "do ordain and establish" were included in the Preamble to the Massachusetts State Constitution in 1780, seven years prior to the drafting of the federal Constitution. The Massachusetts State Constitution was then used as a model[10] for the federal Constitution. The idea of the people as the seat of authority, however, traces back to the Declaration of Independence:

> That to secure these rights, governments are instituted among men, deriving their just powers from the consent of the governed, that whenever any form of government becomes destructive of these ends, it is the right of the people to alter or to abolish it, and to institute new government, laying its foundation on such principles, and organizing its powers in such form, as to them shall seem most likely to effect their safety and happiness. (National Archives)

Self-governance within the context of nation-states is referred to as national sovereignty, which is an important concept in international law. This notion of the people as the source of power and authority became one of the most enduring and inspiring aspects of the new government. This construction and use is the very embodiment of the concept of *popular sovereignty*, where the people rather than a monarch rule. Popular sovereignty brings with it the unique concept that the multitude

10 Other state constitutions also served as models for the federal Constitution, especially with regard to specific aspects of the proposed government's new structure.

of sovereigns (the people) may abolish their government as they choose (Amar 1998). Constitutional scholar, Akhil Reed Amar, has noted that the original document, prior to the addition of the Bill of Rights, makes only one other use of the phrase "the people" and then it is only about the people choosing the members of the House of Representatives.[11] It was later used, to great effect, in Lincoln's Gettysburg Address as the source of devotion for those who fell in battle: " … that government of the people, by the people, for the people shall not perish from the earth."

The end of the second decade (and the beginning of the third) of the 21st century brought new challenges to the definition of "We the People." Attacks on the legitimacy of certain types of immigrants were front and center of those challenges. But, we also turned our attention on those already here. Conflicts between supporters of the Black Lives Matter movement (including those fighting against what they saw as the rise of fascism) and supporters of President Trump's Make America Great movement (sometimes calling themselves America Firsters) like the Proud Boys, the Ku Klux Klan, and others called into question which of them were the rightful heirs to "We the People."[12]

Amanda Gorman (2019), best known now for her viral reading of her poem "The Hill we Climb" at the inauguration of President Joseph R. Biden, Jr., on January 20, 2021, earlier wrote:

> We the people live in a less than perfect union
> That accuses the vulnerable and never the top class and race
> When children are 'illegal' and intolerance bans humans
> I wonder who 'we the people' are in the first place

11 Amar also notes that "the people" appears once again in the very last of the 10 amendments constituting the Bill of Rights. This amendment reserves any powers not explicitly delegated to the national government to the states or to the people. He writes: "The Preamble and the Tenth Amendment are perfect bookends, fittingly the alpha and the omega of the Founders' (revised) Constitution" (1998, 120).

12 While not the central focus of this work, we would assert that those who told lies about the outcome of the 2020 elections and sought to make those lies true through violent insurrection have little, if any, claim to being the rightful heirs. They, however, see it otherwise, that all others, especially those of color and those who take a different political view are the ones to be excluded from the birthright suggested by the Preamble.

Gorman's words are harsh, but no doubt capture and reflect the feelings of some within "we the people" about what their rightful place is or should be. Certainly, the period around 2020 has given many of us pause to consider "who 'we the people' are in the first place." Who is referenced by those three words is significant because, as Justice Stephen Breyer (2010) has noted, they are the "single source of legitimizing power" (xi).

Applying the Approaches to the Preamble

What follows is an attempt to interpret the Preamble to the Constitution in much the same way as legal scholars and justices have done with respect to the rest of the document to determine if law or policy is consistent with it. We should once again stress that this is in no way an attempt to suggest that the Preamble be used to evaluate the constitutionality of a given statute or policy. To understand how different constituencies view the significance of the Preamble, we researched opinions from a professional source (Findlaw.com), a government source (the federal government's U. S. Courts website), and an academic source (Adler and Gorman 1975). In this way, both consistencies and differences in understanding can be quickly highlighted.

According to Findlaw.com (n.d.),

> The preamble states the purpose of the Constitution and the intention of the entire document full of laws. The preamble is not actually a law or a legal document, but it is used to make it clear what to expect in the Constitution. Namely, the preamble says that the Constitution aims to create laws around justice, peace, defense, welfare, liberty, and prosperity for a "more perfect" country for Americans.

This succinct statement discounts the higher purpose of the Preamble (the reason for this book) and instead focuses on the source of the governmental powers outlined in the Constitution.

The federal government's U. S. Courts website (n.d.) states that the Preamble "clearly communicates the intentions of the framers and the purpose of the document" while also making clear that "the preamble is an introduction to the highest law of the land; it is not the law. It does not define government powers or individual rights." This statement clarifies that the Preamble shows the framers' intentions, but also that it does not carry the weight of law. It does however refer to a deeper intent for the Framers than merely introducing the Constitution.

Adler and Gorman (1975), in their deep-dive analysis of the Preamble, note that "the objectives specified in the preamble are ends to be served by the constituted government. The ultimate justification of any act of government, whether legislative, judicial, or executive, should in principle at least reside in the possibility of showing that it serves one or more of the objectives" (78). Their analysis supports the conclusion that the Preamble serves as more than a reminder that the source of federal power is the American people or a clarification that the Preamble does not constitute law. In fact, they state that the Preamble "names six specific objectives which together constitute the common good that is to be served" (77).

Comparing opinions from these sources confirms that the Preamble is far more than an introduction to the Constitution. It is a statement by the Framers of their reasons justifying the formation of a new, independent government. In academic or business terms, it is a *mission statement*. It is the Framers' motivation for fixing the problems in the Articles of Confederation and starting over from scratch, on their own terms, without precedent or guidance. It details the American people's specific requirements for their government, requirements that had not been met either under Colonial rule or in the Articles.

Overview of the Book

Thus far, we have introduced the Preamble and how we will analyze its effectiveness as a guide to more contemporary policy makers and citizens. Having established a foundation of the apparent intent of the Framers, we will move forward to interpret the Preamble in the context of the time at which laws/policies designed to achieve its objectives were adopted. Our focus will be less on history and law, but on more recent policy and whether or not we have lived up to the goals established in the Preamble.

In Chapter Two we will discuss the purpose of government in general and the nature of the objectives government should be expected to address. The argument will be made that the Articles of Confederation had proven insufficient in bringing the colonies together, or for promoting America overseas. Since a primary purpose of the Constitution was to make the Union stronger, it should be a focus of future governments to continue to strengthen the Union. Examples will be offered of laws and policies that both work to support and work against the Union.

Framer, and later President, James Madison (1961a) noted in *Federalist* #51: "Justice is the end of government. It is the end of civil society. It ever has been and ever will be pursued until it be obtained, or until liberty be lost in the pursuit." Chapter Three addresses the issue of justice. Our discussion includes the three dimensions of justice (contributive, commutative, and distributive) and how they are reflected in the Constitution. We offer examples of how issues of justice have been addressed by the government over time and the resulting impacts on society.

In Chapter Four we address the issue of civil peace, which is closely tied to establishing justice (hence the recent protest slogan "No Justice, No Peace"). According to Adler & Gorman (1975, 89), "The undertaking to insure domestic tranquility attempts to ward off the prevalence of acts springing from the vice of injustice." Our discussion will include the delicate balance of public safety and personal liberty as well as the interrelations between the objectives (e.g., the difficulties of maintaining civil peace in an unstable Union, which resulted in the Civil War). Examples will be offered of how different governments dealt with that balance.

"Security against foreign danger is one of the primitive objects of civil society. It is an avowed and essential object of the American union. The powers requisite for attaining it must be effectually confided to the federal councils." (Madison 1961b) Chapter Five will discuss how the defense was intended to be "common" as well as how it should be provided. Our discussion will touch upon the delicate balance of power between the federal government and the states. Issues pertaining to the second amendment will be addressed, and discussion will include how the government has fared in providing a common defense.

Chapter Six will address how the Framers intended the "general welfare" to be promoted. Our discussion will include the modern stigma associated with welfare and how the government, over time, chose to promote the general welfare. We will discuss the struggle to narrowly define "the general welfare," both among the Framers and later in the Supreme Court, and the underlying issue of limited versus unlimited government. Further discussion will include whose welfare the Framers were concerned with versus whose welfare the legislative branch has been promoting in recent decades. Since the power to tax and spend lies with Congress, they have the power to direct taxpayers' funds where they wish. As Robert Reich likes to point out, "The size of government isn't the problem. That's a canard used to hide the far larger problem. The larger problem is that much of government is no longer working for the vast majority it's intended to serve. It's working instead for a small minority at the top" (2014, no page).

Adler & Gorman (1975) quote Charles H. McIlwain (1940): "The two fundamental correlative elements of constitutionalism for which all lovers of liberty must yet fight are the legal limits to arbitrary power and a complete political responsibility of government to the governed" (136). Chapter Seven will discuss the nature of the "blessings of liberty", and how they are to be secured. The Bill of Rights will be discussed in this chapter, as will issues related to representative government. We will discuss issues and events that have pitted the government and its constituents against each other, as well as the relation between law and liberty.

Chapter Eight is where we will make our case that the Preamble to the Constitution serves as a guide to federal policy as well as a scorecard for voters to use to determine which of our representatives are looking out for our best interests. We will tie together everything discussed in the prior chapters to show how we, as voters, can perform our civic duty with an understanding and appreciation for what men like James Madison, Alexander Hamilton and Thomas Jefferson believed Americans were owed by their government. The Framers of our Constitution left us a tool for performing and judging good government; it is in our best interests as Americans to make the most of that tool.

Bibliography

Adler, Mortimer Jerome, and William Gorman. 1975. *The American Testament.* New York: Praeger Publishers.

Amar, Akhil Reed. 1998. *The Bill of Rights: Creation and Reconstruction.* New Haven, CT: Yale University Press.

Amar, Akhil Reed. 2005. "Rethinking Originalism." *Slate.* September 21, 2005. In *The Constitution Today: Timeless Lessons for the Issues of Our Era,* edited by Akhil Reed Amar. New York: Basic Books (an imprint of Perseus Books, subsidiary of Hachette Book Group).

Breyer, Stephen. 2010. *Making our Democracy Work: A Judge's View.* New York: Alfred A. Knopf.

Cohen, Jeffrey. 1986. "The Dynamics of the 'Revolving Door' on the FCC." *American Journal of Political Science* 30(4) (November): 689–708.

Constitution Center, The. n.d. "The Preamble to the Constitution." Constitutioncenter.org. Accessed June 9, 2020, https://constitutioncenter.org/blog/the-preamble-to-the-constitution.

Cornell Law School. n.d. "Strict Construction: Definition from Nolo's Plain-English Law Dictionary." Law.cornell.edu. Accessed June 9, 2020, https://www.law.cornell.edu/wex/strict_construction.

Epstein, Lee J., and Thomas G. Walker. 2020. *Constitutional Law for a Changing America: Institutional Powers and Constraints,* 10th ed. Thousand Oaks: CQ Press (an imprint of SAGE Publications, Inc).

Findlaw.com. n.d. "Preamble to the Constitution." Accessed July 15, 2020, https://www.google.com/url?q=https://constitution.findlaw.com/preamble.html.

Gorman, Amanda. 2019, May 3. "We the people" recited on *Amanpour & Co.* PBS. Accessed May 10, 2021, https://www.pbs.org/wnet/amanpour-and-company/video/amanda-gorman-activist-and-national-youth-poet-laureate/#:~:text=%E2%80%9CWe%20the%20People.,are%20in%20the%20first%20place.

Heclo, Hugh. 1978. "Issue Networks and the Executive Establishment." In *The New American Political System,* edited by Anthony King. Washington, DC: Aei Press.

Jefferson, Thomas. 2009. "Chapter Three: Crumbling Institutions". In *Reason, Justice and Common Sense: A Collection of Essays from the Sierra Sage,* edited by Leonard A. Semas. Carson City, NV: Sierra Sage Publishing.

Madison, James. 1961a. "Federalist #41." In *The Federalist. A Meridian Book,* edited by Jacob E. Cooke. New York: The World Publishing Company.

Madison, James. 1961b. "Federalist #51." In *The Federalist. A Meridian Book,* edited by Jacob E. Cooke, New York: The World Publishing Company.

McIlwain, Charles H. 1940. *Constitutionalism: Ancient and Modern.* Indianapolis: Liberty Fund, 2008. Accessed July 14, 2020, https://oll.libertyfund.org/titles/2145#McIlwain_7850_367.

Miranda v. Arizona 1966 (384 US 436).

Murrill, Brandon J. 2018, March 15. *Modes of Constitutional Interpretation.* Washington: Congressional Research Service.

National Archives, The. 2020. "The Constitution of the United States." Archives.gov. Accessed June 18, 2020, https://www.archives.gov/founding-docs/constitution.

Reich, Robert. 2014, December 24. "It's Not the Size of the Government That's the Problem." *Baltimore Sun*. Retrieved from https://www.baltimoresun.com/opinion/op-ed/bs-ed-reich-government-20141224-story.html.

Sabatier, Paul. 1986. "Top-down and Bottom-up Approaches to Implementation Research: A Critical Analysis and Suggested Synthesis." *Journal of Public Policy* 6(1): 21–48. Retrieved July 10, 2020. www.jstor.org/stable/3998354.

Strauss, David A. 2010. *The Living Constitution*. Chicago: The University of Chicago Law School. September 27. Accessed July 8, 2020, https.uchicago.edu/ne; https://www.lawws/living-constitution.

Toobin, Jeffrey. 2007. *The Nine: Inside the Secret World of the Supreme Court.* New York: Anchor Books (a division of Random House).

Toobin, Jeffrey. 2012. *The Oath: The Obama White House and the Supreme Court.* New York: Doubleday (a division of Random House).

United States Courts. n.d. "The U. S. Constitution: Preamble." Uscourts.gov. Accessed June 9, 2020, https://www.uscourts.gov/about-federal-courts/educational-resources/about-educational-outreach/activity-resources.

Weingast, Barry. 1981. "Regulation, Reregulation, and Deregulation: The Political Foundations of Agency Clientele Relationships." *Law and Contemporary Problems* 44(1): 147–77, doi:10.2307/1191389.

Chapter Two

Form a More Perfect Union

A *more perfect* Union, it could be argued, presupposes that the Union existed before the Constitution. Some have made the argument that the Union is a metaphorical or symbolic one with roots stretching back in time beyond the Articles of Confederation, beyond the Declaration of Independence, beyond any compact made prior to that by the colonies. Hence, the aspirational language, not just to form a union, but *a more perfect union*. Putting the metaphysical and symbolic debate aside, we can trace the beginnings of this more perfect union, first to our separation from Great Britain and second to repairing the flaws in the governmental structure under the Articles of Confederation.

In the Beginning

The birth of the move towards independence came on June 7, 1776, when Richard Henry Lee, the delegate from Virginia to the Second Continental Congress introduced the "Lee Resolution," a proposal for the colonies to declare independence from Great Britain. The resolution, in turn, led to the drafting of the Declaration of Independence, which was the colonies' formal letter of intent to King George III (Our Documents Initiative 2001).

Another eventual outcome from the Lee Resolution was the Articles of Confederation, the colonists' first attempt at a constitution. Ratified by all 13 states in 1781, the Articles of Confederation were the foundation of our government until the Constitution was ratified in June 1788. The story of that Philadelphia Constitutional Convention in 1787 actually began in Virginia in 1785.

Since long before the Articles of Confederation were ratified, Maryland and Virginia had been fighting over control of Chesapeake Bay and the Potomac River. Maryland had closed the Potomac to Virginia's citizens, and Virginia responded by charging Maryland citizens tolls to use the bay. Other states were having trade issues as well, offering justification for a convention of the states to address commerce disputes. At Virginia's General Assembly in October of 1785, John Tyler introduced a resolution inviting commissioners from all 13 states to meet in Annapolis in 1786 to discuss creating a uniform system of commercial regulations. The invitation asked that the commissioners meet in Annapolis on the first Monday of September.

Disappointingly, only five states sent commissioners: New York, New Jersey, Pennsylvania, Delaware and Virginia. Without a quorum, the convention could not realize its ambitions. The commissioners that made the trip to Annapolis, however, knew that there was more to address between the states than simply commerce. They drafted a report, written by Alexander Hamilton, that emphasized the importance of all states meeting to address the issues of trade and commerce. However, one of the states that attended the failed Annapolis convention, New Jersey, had empowered its commissioners to "consider how far an [*sic*] uniform system in their commercial regulations *and other important matters* may be necessary to their common interest and permanent harmony (Ottenberg 1959, 878, emphasis added).

Hamilton used this language in the report to expand the agenda of the coming meeting to "other important matters" that were critical to the state of the Union. Infused with calm and humility, the report suggested a convention in Philadelphia in May of 1787, "to devise such further provisions as shall appear to them necessary to render the

Constitution of the Federal Government adequate to the exigencies of the Union … " Once Congress agreed to the need for a meeting for "the sole and express purpose of revising the Articles of Confederation" (Ottenberg 1959, 882), the Constitutional Convention was born.

It became clear to the Framers that for the country to be successful, both domestically and internationally, the states had to speak with one collective voice, promote one federal agenda. States were imposing tariffs on goods coming from other states. They were also minting their own money. Major action in Congress required the unanimous consent of all states. There was no strength granted to the central government, no ability to respond quickly to events, and no mechanism for the central government to raise money for its efforts except by the grace of the state governments.

To that end, Alexander Hamilton and James Madison lobbied the states to ratify the Constitution; together with John Jay they wrote the *Federalist Papers* under the pseudonym Publius, a series of 85 articles intended to convince New Yorkers to ratify the Constitution. In *Federalist #1*, Alexander Hamilton (1961) makes the opening statement that lays the foundation for their case:

> To the People of the State of New York:
>
> After an unequivocal experience of the inefficiency of the subsisting federal government, you are called upon to deliberate on a new constitution for the United States of America. The subject speaks its own importance; comprehending in its consequences nothing less than the existence of the union, the safety and welfare of the parts of which it is composed, the fate of an empire in many respects the most interesting in the world.

Hamilton saw protecting the Union as the issue of premier importance in ratifying the Constitution. This concern for the strength of the Union was also shared by General George Washington in his farewell letter to the army in 1783:

> There are four things, which I humbly conceive, are essential to the well-being, I may even venture to say, to the existence of the United States as an Independent Power:
>
> 1st. An indissoluble Union of the States under one Federal Head.
>
> 2dly. A Sacred regard to Public Justice.

> 3dly. The adoption of a proper Peace Establishment, and
>
> 4thly. The prevalence of that pacific and friendly Disposition, among the People of the United States, which will induce them to forget their local prejudices and policies, to make those mutual concessions which are requisite to the general prosperity, and in some instances, to sacrifice their individual advantages to the interest of the Community. (Washington 1783)

These four things reflect three of the six objectives listed in the Preamble: forming a more perfect union, establishing justice, and insuring domestic tranquility (the last two both fall within this objective). These were the foremost concerns Washington expressed as he stepped down from his position as head of the common defense.

The Articles of Confederation had failed to bring unity to the states, but rather sowed confusion at home and distrust abroad. Shay's Rebellion and the national government's inability to raise funds sufficient to begin paying down the international debt run up during the War for Independence were among the many examples of the shortcomings of the Articles. The convention in 1787 was intended to find ways to bolster the articles, but instead made it apparent that a total rewrite was needed.

Maintaining the Union through the Civil War

Even seasoned governments struggle with such challenges; one fresh out of the box has no institutional memory, no experience or instinct to use for difficult decisions. Even small challenges can stress a government when they pile up, or when there is difficulty agreeing to a solution. While the new government did in fact face a number of smaller challenges right from the start, it was a significant challenge, one that usually caused voices to elevate and fists to clench, that eventually put the Union to its ultimate test: slavery.

After ratification of the Constitution, divisions remained among the states, much later leading President Lincoln to make the need to maintain a strong union a big part of his first inaugural address in March of 1861. Confederate troops fired on Fort Sumter in Charleston, South Carolina less than six weeks later. It was apparent to the Framers that maintaining a strong and enduring union would be both crucial and challenging – a primary reason why it is mentioned first in the Preamble. They clearly saw the need to work to strengthen the Union as a primary responsibility of the government. Adler and Gorman (1975) explain the struggle the new government faced:

> To whatever extent, then, the activities of an instituted government enlighten and strengthen the basic unity that gives a people its historical existence, to that extent the government is good. On the other hand, a government could have the opposite effect if, in the name of forming a more perfect union, it were to impose a rigidly uniform test of loyalty; or if, panicking about the security of the union, it were to violate liberties that were intended to be immunities from government. (85)

It could easily be argued that the document that followed the Preamble contained compromises and structures that contradicted the stated goals of the Preamble. Naturally, first among these is the 3/5s Compromise, which allowed slave states to count their slaves as 3/5s of a person for the purpose of allocation of seats in Congress and aid from the national government. How could someone counting as only 3/5s of a person be fully included in "We the People"? The larger issue of slavery as a threat to the Union dates back at least as far as the debate over the Declaration of Independence. Southern delegations threatened to walk away from the Continental Congress if a clause condemning the slave trade were not removed. To hold the fractured colonies together the issue of slavery was kicked down the road to whatever new government would follow.

A multitude of legislative battles ensued during the years following 1808, the date set in Article I, section nine of the Constitution for when Congress could legislate regarding slavery. Here again, a compromise was included that pushed consideration of a divisive issue farther down the road. Congress could not act to outlaw the practice, but could raise a small amount of revenue for the national government from it. Throughout the North, the abolition movement spread, while in the South plantation owners and other business owners who relied on the free labor slaves provided in order to turn a profit dug in.

As more and more subsequent compromises failed to achieve the goal of establishing a more perfect union, federal courts became more receptive to the legal argument put forth by southern states that actions taken by the north-dominated Congress infringed upon their rights as sovereign states – the so-called states' rights argument.[1] One such compromise let Maine into the Union as a free state and Missouri to be admitted as a slave state, with no other states created from territories in the Louisiana Purchase north of 36° 30′ to be admitted as slave states. As despicable as our 20/20 historical hindsight may view such a compromise, it seemed to work – at least for a while. The Missouri Compromise was passed in 1820 and lasted until 1854 when it was surpassed by the Kansas-Nebraska Act. In 1857 it was formally declared unconstitutional by the Supreme Court in the Dred Scott decision, in which the Court ruled that Congressional attempts to ban slavery in the territories was beyond the scope of its powers. The decision only served to enrage abolitionists and harden the position of the South. The 1860 election of Abraham Lincoln, the first Republican president, empowered a man whose Party Platform was clearly anti-slavery, but at the same time stated a desire to preserve the Union. Of course, the reaction of southern states to Lincoln's election was swift, with South Carolina being the first to secede.

The North's victory in the ensuing Civil War, accompanied by the passage of the Thirteenth, Fourteenth, and Fifteenth Amendments to the Constitution brought the Union back together. Certainly, during Reconstruction it was anything but perfect and one could argue that the final battle of the War was fought three years later in 1868 through the impeachment of Andrew Johnson,[2] who took a more sympathetic view of the former Confederate States than many of Lincoln's Party would have preferred. Even though Johnson survived the impeachment, being

1 States' rights has been an argument that has been both conservative and liberal (in the modern usage of those terms) depending on the issue. For example, while often associated with the more conservative views on race relations, states' rights was the primary argument used in a dismissed original jurisdiction Supreme Court case challenging the 2020 presidential election (*Texas v Pennsylvania*, et al).

2 Some would argue that we have continued a "cold" civil war ever since and that the January 6, 2021 events were merely a heating up of that continued conflict.

acquitted by the Senate, his victory was so narrow – by a single vote – that he was sufficiently chastened and disabused of any notion that he could seek a term as president in his own right. In fact, Ulysses S. Grant was nominated by the Republicans during the impeachment trial in the Senate. Johnson's own former Party (the Democrats) wanted nothing to do with him since he bolted from their ranks to run with Lincoln in 1864.

Manifest Destiny and Economic Growth

Much of the need for compromises as new states were admitted was attributable to the fact that we were, in fact, growing and needing to admit new states. Naturally, much of this expansion came as the country moved farther west. As early as the presidency of Thomas Jefferson, the nation nearly doubled in size with the addition of approximately 828,000 square miles of land west of the Mississippi River. Eventually, 15 new states would be carved out of the territory.[3] This was the beginning of an expansion all the way to the west coast, along the way annexing territory belonging to Spain and Mexico.

The phrase "Manifest Destiny" came, not from a statement of policy by any president or by legislation in Congress, but from a newspaper editorial in 1845. The term was used to reference our nation's special place in the eyes of God, that this westward expansion was God's will.[4] Later, it would be used with derision by critics of expansion. While some still saw our expansion north to Alaska, west into the Pacific, and southeast into the Caribbean as part of that providential guidance, others saw it as embracing the same kind of imperialism we fought against in

3 A small portion of this land would be ceded by the United States to Canada to create a uniform border across the western states. That small portion of the land became parts of Saskatchewan and Alberta provinces.

4 Julius Pratt (1927) suggests that the phrase may have come from a speech on the floor of the House of Representatives on January 3, 1846 in a debate over our title to Oregon. Pratt also notes that it is likely the phrase was used in an editorial a week earlier (December 27, 1845) in the *Morning News* of New York, written by John O'Sullivan. He also edited another journal associated with the Democratic Party, the *Democratic Review* which touted later (in April of 1859) that O'Sullivan had editorialized in that periodical that the United States was "destined to manifest" democratic principles and "God's natural and moral law" to the world (Pratt 1927, 797).

the Revolutionary War. Lyon Rathbun (2001) suggests that prior to this Oregon question that arose in the mid-1840s, many may have thought our expansion had died with the furor over the annexation of Texas. Rathbun argues it was abolitionists, fearful of the extension of the slave trade into the newly (or about to be) acquired territories, that drove the opposition to territorial expansion. In 1844, Daniel Webster addressed a gathering of citizens in Worcester, MA, regarding his opposition to taking title to Oregon, "Instead of aiming to enlarge its boundaries let us seek, rather, to strengthen its union, to draw out its resources, to maintain and improve its institutions of religion and liberty, and thus to rush it forward in its career of prosperity and glory" (Rathbun 2001, 459). Clearly, Webster thought that strengthening the Union was more important than expanding it.

Certainly, if territorial acquisition can be used as a measure of striving toward perfection then Manifest Destiny contributed to a more perfect union. It most assuredly had its detractors for the roughshod manner in which much of that territory was obtained. To achieve it, Mexicans and Spaniards were pushed aside and Native Americans were completely uprooted and taken from the fertile hunting and farming lands they occupied and unceremoniously left in dry, sometimes inhospitable land and told to fend for themselves.

Hand-in-hand with the nation's (mostly) westward expansion was the onset of the industrial revolution in America. Railroads expanded throughout the existing states and on into the newly acquired territories. Coal and steel were concentrated primarily in the North and contributed to the Union's victory over the Confederacy. What, however, did this rapid industrialization of the country contribute to creating a more perfect union? To this point, Joyce Chaplin (2015) writes, "Within the United States, historians were above all concerned to examine whether the republic, born in revolution and tested in Civil War, had achieved its promises to liberate its citizens—the criteria for historical consequence were defined in terms of justice among human beings" (288). For our discussion, this question she raises can be aimed squarely at the Preamble. Would not a more perfect union "liberate its citizens"?[5]

5 Further on in our discussion we will broach the question she raises with respect to justice.

Chaplin's discussion moves us beyond the turning point in history of the American Revolution and argues that future analysts of the time should focus more on the impact the American version of the Industrial Revolution had on the progress of humanity. Equally, we could argue that the Industrial Revolution would test the very objectives of both the Declaration of Independence and the Preamble.

The more rapid onset of the Industrial Revolution in the north – the Union – contributed to its victory in the Civil War and thus helped to preserve the Union while making it more just, more perfect through the elimination of the slave-driven economy. Many of those newly freed slaves headed north to the manufacturing jobs in the country's urban centers. There they faced conditions not much better than on the plantation, low wages, horrible living conditions, exploitative bosses, and so on. Coupling the rapid technological advances with the growth of capitalism, just as in the plantation oriented southern economy, business owners sought to squeeze every dime of profit they could out of their enterprises, often on the backs of their laborers, both black and white, and sometimes very young.

To be sure, the American Industrial Revolution provided the capital necessary for the country to expand further. But, the desire for that capital created systemic inequity that lasted for decades. It brought pollution, dangerous workplaces, abuse of workers, and eventually vast disparity in income and wealth that some argue would threaten the economic and political infrastructure of the Union, perhaps making it a little less perfect. Those questions, however, deal more directly with the issues of justice (Chapter Three) and domestic tranquility (Chapter Four) later in our discussion.

Political Polarization in the Late 20th and Early 21st Centuries

As part of the process of making course corrections following the impacts of the Civil War and the American Industrial Revolution, our Progressive Era brought changes to both politics and business. We adopted laws that limited the growing power of urban political machines like Tammany Hall in New York City and the Cook County Democratic Committee in Chicago,[6] including civil service reform to limit corrupt hiring practices and the adoption of the direct primary to mitigate the impact on democracy of one-party domination of cities and states. The early 20th Century also brought reforms spearheaded by progressives of both political parties, but perhaps most often associated with the Republican Party because of the efforts and personality of Teddy Roosevelt. These efforts were squarely aimed at the tendency of business toward monopoly. "Trust busting" became the rallying theme that led to such actions as the breakup of Standard Oil and, ironically, the consolidation of the fledgling telecommunications industry into a group of noncompeting local telephone providers, the largest of which was American Telephone and Telegraph (AT&T), as something called "regulated natural monopolies."

Beginning in the late 19th and early 20th centuries, the Supreme Court struggled with these course corrections. In the end, during the administration of Franklin D. Roosevelt, the Court came to see that older interpretations of the Constitution were not working. FDR's response to the Great Depression and the roaring economic engine that followed the second World War created systems and institutions that, it could be argued, took us further along the journey toward a more perfect union. In the years following World War II, we also finally achieved Manifest Destiny with the admission of Hawaii and Alaska into the Union in 1959.

With "Manifest Destiny" achieved, there is the real possibility that in the near future (as we write this in early 2021) the residential parts of the District of Columbia may be granted statehood and similarly, the territory of Puerto Rico may as well. As the nation continues to grow, however. There is a real threat to the union in a phenomenon, not necessarily new but perhaps more virulent than ever – partisan polarization.

6 Of course, neither machine was immediately eliminated and remnants of these two, and others, remain today. The influence of Tammany Hall was felt in New York mayoral elections into the 1960s and the national influence of the Cook County machine – the Daley (for its iconic mayor) machine in its later years – continued to be felt nationally in both the 1960 and 1968 presidential elections.

We are in "a new age of partisanship", suggests Alan Abramowitz (2018). The 21st century has been characterized thus far by ideologically polarized institutions, he argues. Former President Obama in an interview with Bill Cowan of CBS News observed "[t]he one thing that gnaws on me is the degree of continued polarization. It's gotten worse over the last several years" (Wood and Jordan 2017, 2).

Steve Kornacki (2018) of MSNBC has written an astute history of the phenomenon. He posits that it was the arrival of Newt Gingrich as a young firebrand congressman in January of 1979 that kicked off our current polarized politics. Others, including political scientist James Campbell (2018) have suggested that it goes deeper and farther back than Gingrich. A number of political scientists believe a political realignment took place in the mid-1960s over the issue of civil rights (Carmines, Renten, and Stimson 1982) either a complete partisan realignment or one that changed the coalition making up the dominant party of the time – the Democratic Party. The result was conservative southern Democrats leaving their party to become Republicans. Thus, by the time Gingrich showed up, the new battle lines had already been drawn and whatever Democratic office holders remained in the south were there by virtue of the power of incumbency.

The arrival of cable news, talk radio, and later the Internet, served to solidify those battle lines. Close elections, in which the popular vote winner lost, the Great Recession, COVID-19, the social and racial unrest of 2020, and the insurrection of January 6, 2021 have once again stretched the strength of the union.

Is Our Union More Perfect?

By at least one measure – the geographic size of the United States – you could argue that we are more perfect. This is especially the case if you happen to be a believer of the Manifest Destiny ideology. Also, by virtue of being more diverse, through emancipation of slaves and the immigration of a wide range of nationalities, one could argue we are more perfect. Naturally, those in our society who adhere to a philosophy of white supremacy would see this diversity as detracting from our perfection. Have we endured policy mistakes and then corrected them? We believe the answer to be yes, and that would inch us closer to perfection.

Rousseau did not believe in the human being as perfect, but believed in its perfectibility. He was not alone. The treatment of perfection ranges from Aristotle's belief that the pursuit of one's *telos* was perfection in itself to more recent discussions by political philosophers that highlight the application of reason to achieve respect for others. It is not necessarily the case then that that respect is a fixed point, but one that likely moves with human intellectual and emotional growth and thus perfection (or its achievement) is in the pursuit, not the attainment. The same could be said of the United States, that we are not perfect, but our virtue lies in our perfectibility. A look back at 2020 and early 2021 tells us nothing, if not that we still have a long way to go. Yet, we continue, even as we often experience steps backwards, to improve our lot, even if in small ways.

Bibliography

Abramowitz, Alan. 2018. *The Great Alignment: Race, Party Transformation, and the Rise of Donald Trump.* New Haven, CT: Yale University Press.

Adler, Mortimer Jerome, and William Gorman. 1975. *The American Testament.* New York: Praeger Publishing.

Campbell, James E. 2018. *Polarized: Making Sense of a Divided America.* Princeton, NJ: Princeton University Press.

Carmines, Edward G., Steven H. Renten, and James A. Stimson. 1984. "Events and Alignments: The Party Image Link." In *Controversies in Voting Behavior,* 2nd ed., edited by Richard G. Niemi and Herbert F. Weisberg. Washington, DC: Congressional Quarterly Press.

Chaplin, Joyce. 2015. "The Other Revolution." *Early American Studies* 13(2) (Spring): 285–308.

Hamilton, Alexander. 1961. "Federalist #1." In *The Federalist. A Meridian Book,* edited by Jacob E. Cooke. . New York: The World Publishing Company.

Kornacki, Steve. 2018. *The Red and the Blue: The 1990s and the Birth of Political Tribalism.* New York: HarperCollins.

Ottenberg, Louis. 1959. "A Fortunate Fiasco: The Annapolis Convention of 1786." *American Bar Association Journal* 45(8): 834–37, 877–82.

Our Documents Initiative, The. 2001. "Lee Resolution (1776)." Ourdocuments.gov. Accessed June 18, 2020, https://www.ourdocuments.gov/doc.php?flash=false&doc=1.

Pratt, Julius W. 1927. "The Origin of 'Manifest Destiny'." *The American Historical Review* 32(4): 795–98.

Rathbun, Lyon. 2001. "The Debate over Annexing Texas and the Emergence of Manifest Destiny." *Rhetoric and Public Affairs* 4(3) (Fall): 459–94.

Washington, George. 1783. "Washington's Circular Letter of Farewell to the Army, June 8, 1783." Washington: Library of Congress. Accessed June 20, 2020, https://www.loc.gov/item/mgw434172/.

Wood, B. Dan, and Soren Jordan. 2017. *Party Polarization in America: The War over Two Social Contracts*. New York: Cambridge University Press.

Chapter Three

Establish Justice

As with all of the goals set forth in the Preamble, but perhaps to a greater extent, establishing justice has been a difficult target. As the definition of "we the people" has grown, our ability to provide justice for that ever-growing and diversifying population has had a hard time catching up. This is even more the case when you consider that on the list of priorities, second to the need to maintain a strong union was the need for the even administration of justice. The Articles of Confederation made no provision for the establishment of national courts, creating conflicts among the states as to how justice was administered. These conflicts were viewed as an indication of weakness by foreign nations. Thus the need to establish justice was viewed as vital by those attending the federal Convention of 1787. Adler and Gorman stated it well:

> Almost as important as concern for the precarious kind of unity that gives a society its very *being* is concern for the quality of the interactions among persons that give society its *life*. It is for this reason that a constitutional government should aim at establishing justice. (1975, 85)

Aspects of Justice

Adler and Gorman go on to describe theories of justice that recognize three different sets of relationships among members of a society:

- The duties or obligations that individuals in a society have with respect to that society (contributive justice),
- The rights and duties that are borne by individuals in a society with respect to other individuals (commutative justice), and
- The obligations a society has with respect to the rights possessed by its individual members (distributive justice).

They also make the argument that justice can be seen as the primary objective of government, the one without which the other objectives cannot be attained. To make their case they quote James Madison (1961) from *Federalist #51*: "Justice is the end of government. It is the end of civil society. It ever has been and ever will be pursued until it be obtained, or until liberty be lost in the pursuit" (1975, 86).

When a government provides its constituents with what is rightly theirs, that government is providing distributive justice, treating each person fairly. Fairly, however, does not necessarily mean equally, particularly in social and economic terms. This is the point made by Robert Nozick in his classic work *Anarchy, State, and Utopia* (1974). According to Nozick, economic inequality is not necessarily a bad thing, but if the unequal distribution came about as a result of unfair rules or practices, it might be necessary to have government intervene. Such intervention should be intended to protect individuals from unfair distributions resulting from ill-gotten gains: fraud, theft, or force. Michael Sandel (2009) explains how John Rawls' Difference Principle permits certain inequalities in principle in order to compensate for other inequities. He does this by proposing a "veil of ignorance" for all participants so that no information advantage exists. Under those conditions, what principles would we choose to apply in governing for social and economic inequalities?

> To guard against the risk of finding ourselves in crushing poverty, we might at first thought favor an equal distribution of income and wealth. But then

> it would occur to us that we could do better, even for those on the bottom. Suppose that by permitting certain inequalities, such as higher pay for doctors than for bus drivers, we would improve the situation of those who have the least – by increasing access to health care for the poor. Allowing for this possibility, we would adopt what Rawls calls "the difference principle": only those social and economic inequalities are permitted that work for the benefit of the least advantaged members of society. (151–2)

However, the government also has an obligation to see to it that the members of society treat each other fairly. This is referred to as commutative justice, which Gunneman (1985) explains is "rooted in the fundamental moral prohibition against harm" (102). This is close to, but not exactly the same as, Mill's notion of the harm principle, in which he asserts: "The only purpose for which power can be rightly exercised over any member of a civilized community against his will, is to prevent harm to others" (Mill 1859 in Collini 1989, 13). The application of the principle is to regulate the intersection of private actions with others in society. While some see this as individual license for antisocial behavior and use of one's property, we believe Mill intended it as a mechanism by which individuals control their own behavior, and absent that, that government would be justified in limiting such conflicts.[1] It is this form of justice which Adler and Gorman believe the framers were referring to in the Preamble. Their case is compelling.

> Commutative justice involves correlative rights and duties – rights that one individual claims for himself and demands that others respect, and duties on the part of others to respect those rights – for example, an individual's right to security of life and limb; his right against the invasion of his privacy or arbitrary intrusion in his home; his right against defamation of character; his rights with regard to the acquirement, accumulation, exchange, and conveyance of property. When such rights are legally acknowledged, the laws impose upon all the obligation to respect them. Whereas distributive justice consists in those measures by which the state or organized society renders

1 An oft-cited example is the way in which you make use of your property to gain the most pleasure from it, but that derivation of pleasure denies your neighbor the ability to derive pleasure from their property. Imagine if there were no land use (zoning) laws and you attempted to put a McDonald's Drive Thru in your driveway. This action would infringe upon your neighbor's ability to enjoy their yard.

to each person what is rightfully due him, commutative justice consists in one individual's rendering to another what is due him or is his by right. (1975, 86–7)

Larsen and Lawson (2013) make note of the role that the concept of commutative justice should have in discussions of policy, particularly with regard to the evaluation of fairness in agreements and exchanges. They write: "reference to commutative justice can also be found in the right to safety and the right to privacy" (521). We see this in contemporary interpretations of the Constitution protecting reproductive rights and in the creation of agencies like the Consumer Product Safety Commission. From this perspective, one could argue that it is the government's responsibility to motivate its citizenry to treat each other fairly and with respect, or, what has been the more common case, to demotivate its citizenry from treating each other unfairly or with disrespect. Laws *tend* to be written to punish those who behave poorly rather than to motivate people to behave kindly, since our society seems to be more inclined to judge those we deem guilty rather than to persuade people to be considerate (laws tend to utilize the stick rather than the carrot).

The strength of the Union was threatened by the inconsistency with which justice was administered across the states; punishments, and even laws themselves, were devised by local authorities to satisfy the wants and needs of their local populace, and thus what behavior was deemed wrong and what punishment one was given for such behavior varied based on where one was standing when the infraction was committed (vestiges of this remain to this day). Many laws were aimed at taming the behavior of slaves, servants or children, and punishments ranged from shame or humiliation to whipping or the pillory. Crimes against religion were common; blasphemers could be made to stand on a gallows wearing a noose, or be whipped, or be put into the pillory, or even to have a hole burned into their tongue with a red-hot iron (The Law Library n.d.). Laws against skipping church services or even traveling on Sundays proliferated. National laws that create national standards are aimed at creating a level playing field and to minimize state to state differences. The 14th Amendment was the first truly concrete step in this direction.

These inconsistencies would eventually make our new nation look weak and fragile, and would sow unrest among our own population. As historians have noted, there were a great many weaknesses stemming from the Articles of Confederation, which prioritized state power, and state preference, over the needs of national consistency. A weak, or non-existent, executive, no power to tax, the inability to regulate commerce, the competition among states for the coining of money and relations with foreign powers, and an overall lack of coherent policy, especially regarding the meaning and application of justice were among the motivating factors for the calling of the Constitutional Convention – initially to amend the Articles of Confederation – and its eventual scrapping of the Articles entirely. While some delegates argued to leave the application of justice via the courts up to the states, those that sought greater uniformity and didn't trust the state courts to interpret the national constitution won the debate, but lacked a fully formed plan for that court system.

Even today one could argue that justice is not served when states adopt contradictory policies or execute national policy in an uneven manner. The public debate over same sex marriage and the way in which it was resolved reflects the eventual evolution of the policy to provide justice, but in the end it took clarification by the Supreme Court to get us closer to equal justice. So too, the differences in implementing abortion policy, aspects of the Affordable Care Act (ACA or Obamacare), and the differences in public health policy in response to the COVID-19 pandemic, among many others, are recent examples of the uneven distribution of justice.

Contributive justice, on the other hand, is less stick and more carrot; here we see terms like "the common good." Thomas Paine (2017) wrote that the term republic stems from the phrase *res publica,* which loosely translates to *the public good*. Contributive justice stems from the bond between an individual and their community, so that the individual looks out for the common good, while the community looks out for the rights of the individual. In fact, the rights the individual lays claim to are based upon the contribution the individual makes to their community. Michael Sandel (2009) put it this way, contributive justice is about "an opportunity to win the social recognition and esteem that goes with producing what others need and value"

The basis for contributive justice is thus public virtue, or the virtue of people as citizens. It requires a spirit of volunteerism which some Americans do not seem to share. The notion of contributive justice is most often attributed to the work of Gomberg (2007), who argued that complex, interesting work tends to allow workers to achieve satisfaction and recognition and esteem – not unlike the notions expressed in Maslow's hierarchy of needs. On the flip side of that argument is that when the most satisfying work is concentrated in the hands of a few and limiting equality of opportunity that is contributive injustice. Gomberg links this satisfaction to the idea that we, as individuals, are more of what we do than the physical or monetary things we get from work. At the time of this writing, there is tremendous debate in politics and in the media about the requirement to wear a face mask while out in public to help prevent the spread of the Coronavirus. The debate is split along party lines, with Democrats pushing for requiring masks as recommended by the health experts, and Republicans claiming that the masks do not prevent the spread or that the Coronavirus is not as dangerous as the media claim. It is a classic battle of individual rights versus the common good.

Achieving the Goal of Justice

This particular goal in the Preamble is not just at the core of American politics or American life, but it is central to the concept of all constitutional democracies. In an article from 1985, as a follow up to his book, *A Theory of Justice* (1971), Rawls notes:

> In justice as fairness, social unity is understood by starting with the conception of society as a system of cooperation between free and equal persons. Social unity and the allegiance of citizens to their common institutions are not founded on their all affirming the same conception of the good, but on their publicly accepting a political conception of justice to regulate the basic structure of society. (249)

Issues of justice continue to plague all democracies beyond just our country. Here, this notion of justice as fairness often manifests itself at the core of conflicts over systemic racism. For example, *The Washington Post* Police Shootings Database reports that, on average over the period 2015 to mid-2020, the rate at which Black Americans were being killed by police was more than twice that of White Americans (31 per million vs. 13 per million), despite the fact that White Americans outnumbered Black Americans by almost five to one (*The Washington Post*). This is an issue of both commutative justice (mistreatment of Black Americans by other citizens) and distributive justice (mistreatment of Black Americans by their police force and the courts). The issue of distributive justice will be discussed further in Chapter Six, Promote the General Welfare.

Certainly, attempting to achieve justice implies that it has not yet been achieved, and may never be. But, that is not necessarily the point of its inclusion in the Preamble. Establishing justice is, at its very core, an ongoing process. Conditions will always arise, human character will always be weak, and thus there will always be the need to continue to strive for justice. We see the establishment of justice, not as a one shot deal, but as the start of this ongoing process. Societal justice then is rarely, if ever perfect, but as Rousseau and Aristotle saw, it is a part of the process of human perfectibility.

Bibliography

Adler, Mortimer Jerome, and William Gorman. 1975. *The American Testament.* New York: Praeger.

Gomberg, Paul. 2007. *How to Make Opportunity Equal: Race and Contributive Justice,* 1st ed. Malden: Blackwell Publishing.

Gunnemann, John P. 1985. "Capitalism and Commutative Justice." *The Annual of the Society of Christian Ethics* 5: 101–22.

Larsen, Gretchen, and Rob Lawson. 2013. "Consumer Rights: An Assessment of Justice." *Journal of Business Ethics* 112(3) (February): 515–28.

Law Library, The. n.d. "Colonial Period: Criminal Law." Law.jrank.org. Accessed July 7, 2020, https://law.jrank.org/pages/11881/Colonial-Period-Criminal-law.html#:~:-text=Many%20of%20the%20early%20colonial,slaves%2C%20and%20youth%20in%20line.&text=Other%20laws%20punished%20colonists%20for,even%20banned%20traveling%20on%20Sundays.

Madison, James. 1961. "Federalist #51." In *The Federalist.* A Meridian Book, edited by Jacob E. Cooke. New York: The World Publishing Company.

Mill, John Stuart. 1859. "On Liberty." In *J. S. Mill: On Liberty and Other Writings*, edited by Stefan Collini, 1989. New York: Cambridge University Press.

Nozick, Robert. 1974. *Anarchy, State, and Utopia*. New York: Basic Books.

Paine, Thomas. 2017. *Collected Writings: Common Sense/The Crisis/Rights of Man/The Age of Reason*. Scotts Valley: CreateSpace Independent Publishing Platform.

Rawls, John. 1985. "Justice as Fairness: Political not Metaphysical." *Philosophy & Public Affairs* 14(3) (Summer): 223–51.

Sandel, Michael J. 2009. *Justice: What's the Right Thing to Do?* New York: Farrar, Straus and Giroux.

The Washington Post. 2021. Police Shootings Database. Washingtonpost.com. Updated February 18. Accessed February 22, 2021, https://www.washingtonpost.com/graphics/investigations/police-shootings-database/.

Chapter Four

Insure Domestic Tranquility

The year 2020 will long be remembered as the year of the Coronavirus, due to the havoc the virus wreaked around the globe. Our planet had not seen a global pandemic in a century, and so by 2020 few who survived the 1918–20 pandemic were still alive. While the global pandemic experts had some idea of what could happen, the rest of us had to learn about it from our chosen sources for news. 2020 was also a presidential election year in the U. S., and the incumbent president, Donald Trump, obfuscated the facts relating to the pandemic and used divisive rhetoric to inflame support among his loyal followers. One main area of contention was the use of surgical masks to protect against spreading the virus. The healthcare scientists all supported the use of masks as a way to protect others, while President Trump made a point of not wearing a mask while campaigning, with few exceptions. The president supported the rights of the individual to reject the mask, rather than support the wearing of the mask for the public good.

Civil unrest was also a hallmark of 2020 when the issue of racism came to a boil, globally but most fiercely in the United States. The shootings of Breonna Taylor, Ahmaud Aubrey and Rayshard Brooks, and in particular the tortuous death of George Floyd, sparked both small riots and large peaceful protests promoted by such organizations as Black Lives Matter (BLM). The closing of the economy during the spring of 2020 freed many people up to demonstrate publicly their outrage at the systemic racism displayed in many other facets of American culture; employment, education, housing, and credit. Black Americans have felt mistreated by the government throughout America's history, and what had been a slow simmer finally came to a boil in 2020. The slogan used by the BLM protesters gets to the heart of their complaint: no justice, no peace.

The levels of inequality in both income and wealth have been a lively source of discussion ever since the publication of Capital in the Twenty-First Century by Thomas Piketty (2015). The Occupy Wall Street movement which began in New York's financial district in 2011 was a protest on economic inequality, but it expanded later to include protest on political corruption and corporate governance. Robert Reich, in the documentary *Inequality for All* (Chaiken and Dungan 2013), shows the sobering parallels between the U. S. economy in 2010 and earlier in 1928, just before the crash of the stock market and the Great Depression. During his tenure in office, Donald Trump boasted about the strength of the U. S. economy based mostly on strong stock market runs (interspersed with remarkably bad stock market falls), while at the same time minimum wage workers in the U. S. were unable to afford rental housing (Favre 2019).

Our History of Civil Unrest

Such unrest was not new for the United States. In the 1960s dissent over the war in Vietnam and the Civil Rights movement caused cities and college campuses to ignite in protest. As a result of the seemingly endless violence, President Johnson appointed a commission – The Commission on the Causes and Prevention of Violence – following the unrest that came as a result of the assassinations of Martin Luther King, Jr., and Bobby Kennedy. Denenberg notes "Political demonstrations were turning from peaceful marching to street brawling, and, in the aftermath of the ghetto riots, the Black Panthers were talking of urban guerrilla warfare" (1971, 76). History professors and political science faculty often teach students about the protests in the streets of Chicago at the 1968 Democratic National Convention that turned violent and bloody. The Commission's task was to search for the source of such violence and to offer solutions. Denenberg relates that the Commission offered no new data on the recent violence, but placed it squarely in the context of a violent national history. That is, we were a nation of immigrants who pushed the natives out of their territory, faced the brutal conditions of nature on the frontier, turned to lynchings as a form of vigilante justice (racially motivated "justice"), confrontations between labor and management, and much more. Yet, as poor a job as the Commission did in uncovering the real roots of the problem, its appointment was nonetheless an attempt by Johnson to live up to the goal of insuring domestic tranquility.

Just over one hundred years earlier, Lincoln, as well, used an imperfect tool for living up to this objective of the Preamble. While it is easily argued that Lincoln's prosecution of the Civil War might best fit in the category of a more perfect union, his short term use of violence was also an attempt at restoring domestic tranquility. It is doubtful that anyone would, or could, argue that Lincoln did not pursue the War with vigor and ferocity. Yet, when it was coming to its close, it was evident he had what historian Michael Beschloss called a "desire for a gentle peace" (2018, 229). In evidence of that desire, Beschloss offered the words from Lincoln's second inaugural address: "With malice toward none, with charity for all … to do all which may achieve and cherish a just and lasting peace *among ourselves* and with all nations" (2018, 229, emphasis added). Certainly, Lincoln's benevolence toward the Confederate soldiers is a demonstration of his attempts to regain domestic tranquility. Another presidential historian, Doris Kearns Goodwin (2018) reported that Lincoln's "face glowed with approval" upon hearing General Grant's report about letting the soldiers surrendering at Appomattox leave unmolested and allowing the officers to keep their horses and personal firearms. Goodwin notes that Grant, and presumably Lincoln, sought to avoid "unnecessary humiliation" in the hopes officers and soldiers would be more willing to rejoin the Union upon their return home. It is clear that though the War was inevitable, Lincoln sought to return to a condition of domestic tranquility.

Balancing Order and Freedom to Achieve Tranquility

To be sure, what Lincoln did went beyond an everyday interpretation of this particular phrase from the Preamble and borders on national security claims (see Chapter Five on providing a common defense); the two goals are closely related. However, an argument could be made that the simplest perspective on domestic tranquility is but a question of law and order.[1] That "to insure domestic tranquility" the national government needs to enforce laws that keep the peace, that protect persons and property from the evil actions of others.[2] Yet, domestic tranquility is more than simply law and order. Falkenes (1993) notes that in distinguishing himself from the "law and order" rhetoric of his predecessor, Nixon, President Ford sought to emphasize domestic tranquility and to recognize law and order as simply one part of the overall concept. For Ford, according to Falkenes, domestic tranquility was about finding the balance between respect for the law and "fundamental liberties." Thus, government also needs to maintain a rule of law, one where no one is above the law and all are treated equal under that law. To enforce the law without respecting all of the law, such as the individual rights and liberties even the most evil-minded among us retain, does not lead to the attainment of this particular goal. It is in this respect, this balance, that civil peace is established.

For civil peace to be established, other circumstances must also prevail: the union must be strong, the people must feel that they can attain justice, they must feel safe from foreign attacks, they must feel secure in

1 In fact, we make that argument in Chapter Seven using the words of John Locke, James Wilson, and Adler and Gorman.

2 Ragsdale (2013) notes that there are those who argue that domestic tranquility is inexorably linked to the protection of property, but applies the "harm principle" to restrict an individual's enjoyment of that property. That is, you have the right to use and enjoy your property up to the point that "it causes an unreasonable interference with the use and enjoyment of another" (647).

their welfare, and they must have liberty. If any of these other circumstances are in jeopardy, some degree of civil unrest is likely. Civil peace is achieved by pursuing the common good.

Civil peace is also closely related to, but separate from, justice. As Adler and Gorman (89) point out, "The undertaking to establish justice presumes the prevalence in the people of the personal virtue of justice … The undertaking to insure domestic tranquility attempts to ward off the prevalence of acts springing from the vice of injustice." Much of the civil unrest associated with the BLM movement stems from the historical injustices that Black Americans have endured during our country's history. White Americans who do not have experience with the justice system may find it difficult to identify with this problem or even appreciate that it exists, while conservative sources, including President Trump, have protected the status quo by attacking the BLM movement as "'thugs' and 'terrorists,' warning that 'when the looting starts, the shooting starts'" (Serwer 2020). Finding the common good, let alone achieving it, is challenging under these conditions. However, as Adam Serwer opines, these conditions can bring about a moment, an awakening, that can develop along the lines of similar past movements:

> American history has produced a few similar awakenings. In 1955, the images of a mutilated Emmett Till helped spark the civil-rights movement. In 2013, the acquittal of Trayvon Martin's killer inspired Alicia Garza to declare that Black lives matter, giving form to a movement dedicated to finishing the work begun by its predecessors. Just as today, the stories and images of shattered Black lives inspired Americans to make the promises of the Declaration of Independence more than just a fable of the founding. But almost as quickly, the dream of remaking society faltered, when white Americans realized what they would have to sacrifice to deliver freedom. The urgent question now is whether this time is different. (2020)

Adler and Gorman make the point that "To insure domestic tranquility without encroaching upon liberties is a delicate assignment for the constitutional government of a free society" (90). Any efforts to improve conditions for one group are likely to be ill received by another. Under these circumstances, improving conditions for any group will be a function of which group is in power. The common good is, at its heart, a numbers game; it is about which policies do the most good for the most people. That, in turn, is a function of the demographics of the people under consideration. The Grey power movement, for example, came about when America's Baby Boomers began to reach retirement age. Thus the common good of a generation will tend to change in step with the demographics of its constituency. One of the biggest challenges America currently faces is the fact that its demographics are shifting in such a way that cultural groups that were formerly minorities are now taking on majority proportions, and White Americans are becoming a minority. As a result, our country is going through an identity crisis.

The dynamics of these demographic shifts work against the goal of social union, which Adler and Gorman opine are closely related to civil peace: "Without the bonds of union and the tranquility of orderly life, a society would hardly exist as such and would be unable to pursue any purpose in a sustained fashion" (89). The political division currently existing in America has been developing for decades, and has been laid bare by the increasingly raucous debate in Congress, the dearth of scandals occurring in all modern presidential administrations except for the two-term Obama administration, and the unwillingness to compromise across the parties, resulting in little change in the conditions for the American people.

Actively Undermining Domestic Tranquility

Americans' distrust in government has been earned throughout much of its history. The Pew Center for Research (2019) reports on polling data from the American National Election Studies from 1958 to 2019 and notes that since the measure for trust in government reached a high point of 77% in 1964, it has fallen rather steadily since. Two major upticks in the data occurred, both of which were at what political scientists call rally points, in this case over the war in Iraq under George H.W. Bush and after 9/11 under George W. Bush. Utilizing that long-term distrust was one of the most effective tools in the 2016 and 2020 presidential elections, as well as the 2018 midterm elections. It was designed specifically to foment distrust among the voters in the media and in the opposing political party: disinformation, otherwise referred to as "alternative facts" or "fake news." Starting with the size of the crowd at President Trump's 2017 inauguration (and through the briefings on COVID-19), Trump and many of his supporters in the Republican Party chose the path of what Trump Adviser Kellyanne Conway called "alternative facts." Trump, himself, would often use the expression "fake news" for stories in the media that contradicted his world view. While the reference began as a taunt and an attempt to discredit the mainstream media, he even started to use it against media outlets like Fox News when they began (at least in their news shows) to push back against the President's outright lies, especially regarding the outcome of the 2020 election. No doubt, this strategy by Trump and his Republican supporters further undermined Americans' trust in government as well as the media.

Even with Trump out of office the Republican party continued to use his tactics. In mid-February 2021 an arctic blast hit more than a third of the country with subzero temperatures and heavy snows. Texas was particularly hard hit, and particularly unprepared for it. While the entire Texas energy grid was having issues, with more than half of the state having no power, Texas governor Greg Abbott decided it was an opportunity to attack alternative energy sources. Texas' energy grid included a number of wind turbines and solar farms that were expected to provide about 10% of the state's winter energy needs, the rest being provided by natural gas, petroleum, nuclear energy and coal. In an attempt to dodge blame for decades of neglect to his state's infrastructure by his party, Abbott, a Republican, used an interview on the *Hannity* show to push back against the Green New Deal, a progressive policy that has not yet been enacted: "So this shows how the Green New Deal would be a deadly deal for the United States of America"; "It just shows that fossil fuel is necessary for the state of Texas as well as other states to make sure we'll be able to heat our homes in the winter time and cool our homes in the summer time" (Hannity 2021). Abbott implied that the failure of the wind turbines was responsible for the entire power grid issue, which was simply not true. Texas had been neglecting the necessary investment into the state's power grid to protect it from severe cold weather. Former Senator Claire McCaskill, on the *Morning Joe* show on MSNBC February 17, 2021, claimed that the governor had the opportunity to pass legislation requiring that the power grid be upgraded for winter weather, but that he declined to do so since he believes in deregulation (*Morning Joe* 2021).

In the midst of a power crisis among more than half of his state's citizens, Governor Abbott chose to mislead his constituency about the source of the problem – he chose to misrepresent the facts rather than represent his constituents. Similarly Congressman Dan Crenshaw tweeted: "This is what happens when you force the grid to rely in part on wind as a power source. When weather conditions get bad as they did this week, intermittent renewable energy like wind isn't there when you need it" (Lewis 2021). Congressman Crenshaw chose not to lead on behalf of his constituents and instead showed a preference for misleading them. The Electric Reliability Council of Texas (ERCOT), which supplies approximately 90% of the state of Texas' power, reported that "Of the power shortfall that hit Texas, over 80% was due to problems at coal- and gas-fired plants" (Lewis 2021).

It could easily be argued that this lack of trust and its nurturing by elected officials and those seeking office lies at the heart of civil unrest, and thus creates the potential for a lack of domestic tranquility. A certain amount of civil unrest – peaceful protest – is expected in and is a healthy part of any democratic society. However, the fanning of its flames by demagogic politicians only serves to undermine domestic tranquility and make the field fertile for those seeking authoritarian solutions. This would be the case if the policy aims were from either the political right or left.

Returning to Domestic Tranquility

In this chapter we have laid out a broad range of circumstances where elected representatives have fallen short of the mark in terms of leading or even simply representing the interests of their constituents. Certainly, in the cases where policy failures led to civil unrest, and in some cases to actual violence, those same officials failed to live up to the objectives of the Preamble. Even in the recent case of Texas' power grid failure and its denial by some political leaders, while there may not have been unrest or violence, it is hard to claim that it served domestic tranquility.

To be sure, the civil unrest that grew out of various circumstances in 2020 was, no doubt, justified, but equally so were concerns many others had for safety. This is the essence of the balance that is necessary for a government to maintain domestic tranquility, what President Ford referred to as "fundamental liberties." Recall that Ford wanted respect for all of the law, not just order. Such a view is consistent with the words of Founder and Framer, Ben Franklin who famously said, "Those who would give up essential Liberty, to purchase a little temporary Safety, deserve neither Liberty nor Safety."

Bibliography

Adler, Mortimer Jerome, and William Gorman. 1975. *The American Testament*. New York: Praeger Publishers.

Beschloss, Michael. 2018. *Presidents of War: The Epic Story, From 1807 to Modern Times*. New York: Crown Publishing.

Chaiken, Jen and Sebastian Dungan (Producers) and Jacob Kornbluth (Director). 2013. *Inequality for All* [Motion Picture]. United States: 72 Productions.

Denenberg, Richard. 1971. "To Establish Justice, To Insure Domestic Tranquility." *Modern Law Review* 34(1): 75–80.

Falkenes, George T. 1993. "Domestic Tranquility: President Ford's Policy Positions on Criminal Justice Issues." *Presidential Studies Quarterly* 23(3), The Domestic and Foreign Policy Presidencies: 519–32.

Favre, Lauren. 2019, June 20. "Minimum Wage Workers Can't Afford Housing." *U. S. News & World Report*. Retrieved, www.usnews.com.

Goodwin, Doris Kearns. 2018. *Leadership: Lessons from the Presidents for Turbulent Times*. New York: Simon and Schuster.

Hannity. 2021. Interview with Gov. Greg Abbott of Texas. FoxNews.com. Accessed February 17, 2021, https://www.foxnews.com/shows/hannity.

Lewis, Sophie. 2021. "Don't Blame Wind Turbines for Texas' Historic Power Outages." Cbsnews.com. Accessed February 17, 2021, https://www.cbsnews.com/news/wind-power-turbine-texas-power-outage-winter-storm-electrical-grid/.

Morning Joe, 2021. [TV programme] MSNBC. Interview with Claire McCaskill. Accessed February 27, 2021, https://www.msnbc.com/morning-joe.

Pew Center for Research. 2019. "Public Trust in Government, 1958 to 2019. Accessed February 27, 2021, https://www.pewresearch.org/politics/2019/04/11/public-trust-in-government-1958-2019/

Piketty, Thomas. 2015. *Capital in the Twenty-First Century*. Cambridge, MA: Belknap Press.

Ragsdale, John W., Jr. 2013. "To Return from Where We Started: A Revisioning of Property, Land Use, Economy, and Regulation in America." *The Urban Lawyer* 45(3) (Summer): 631–92.

Serwer, Adam. 2020. "The New Reconstruction." *The Atlantic*. October. Accessed February 27, 2021, https://www.theatlantic.com/magazine/archive/2020/10/the-next-reconstruction/615475/.

Chapter Five

Provide for the Common Defense

Of all the items on the Framers' list of objectives, few would argue at the inclusion of safety, regardless of their position on the political spectrum. At present, however, there is likely to be disagreement over which specific threats are conspiracy theories and which are of real concern. Certainly, what constitutes the means by which a common defense has evolved over the course of history, both in terms of the perceived need for a standing military and the expansion beyond the simple "army and navy" specified in the main body of the Constitution to include an air force. Not even the great inventor of the founding eras – Benjamin Franklin – would have conceived of an air force, let alone a space force.

Framers Make the Case for a Common Defense

In *Federalist #3* John Jay (1961) declared "Among the many objects to which a wise and free people find it necessary to direct their attention, that of providing for their safety seems to be the first." While the framers appreciated that the defense needed to be provided against enemies both foreign and domestic, there were questions pertaining as to how the defense would be "common," where the authority to provide for the defense would be placed within the constitutional powers, and how that authority could be kept in check in case the tools of defense were used to threaten other objectives, such as liberty. James Madison (1961) made this case in *Federalist #41*:

> The veteran legions of Rome were an overmatch for the undisciplined valor of all other nations and rendered her the mistress of the world. Not the less true is it, that the liberties of Rome proved the final victim to her military triumphs; and that the liberties of Europe, as far as they ever existed, have, with few exceptions, been the price of her military establishments. A standing force, therefore, is a dangerous, at the same time that it may be a necessary, provision. On the smallest scale it has its inconveniences. On an extensive scale its consequences may be fatal. On any scale it is an object of laudable circumspection and precaution.

The balance of defensive power between government and its citizenry is an essential question that continues to be a source of division between the major political parties. The issue of who has the right or responsibility to defend the American people was addressed by George Mason (1776) in the Virginia Declaration of Rights, which was adopted by the Virginia Constitutional Convention in June of 1776. The opening phrase in section 13 is familiar:

> That a well-regulated militia, composed of the body of the people, trained to arms, is the proper, natural, and safe defense of a free state; that standing armies, in times of peace, should be avoided as dangerous to liberty; and that in all cases the military should be under strict subordination to, and governed by, the civil power.

It is easy to see the similarity between the opening phrase of this section of the Virginia Constitution and the Second Amendment of the later written and adopted U.S. Constitution. Since James Madison was likely the author of much of the Bill of Rights and he, no doubt, had great familiarity with his home state's constitution, the similarity is likely more than a coincidence. We note, however, that the Virginia document is much clearer with regard to the concept of a standing military, especially in times of peace, and relying more heavily on militias, which could be called into service when needed, as Hamilton also noted in *Federalist #8* (1961a).

From Militias to the National Guard

Interestingly, historian Michael Beschloss (2018) notes that "As one of the chief architects of the American system, Madison knew that the nature of the first major war to be fought under any President [*sic*] would do much to shape how often and how lightly the nation went to war in the future … " (60). The Founders and the Framers were well aware of the precedents they were setting once they began to manipulate the levers of the mechanism of government they had created.[1] So too, even before he became president, George Washington helped to set the standard for civilian control of the military. Many have noted Washington's similarity to the Roman legend, Cincinnatus. Washington, like Cincinnatus, it could be argued rode to rescue a beleaguered army and eventually led that army to victory. While never given the title of dictator, as Cincinnatus was, Washington followed him in voluntarily stepping down from command and retiring to Mount Vernon. Thomas E. Ricks notes, "It was a magnificent deed of renunciation and was recognized as such at the time" (2020, 176). Some have suggested that Washington could have kept his command, and if he desired it could have been installed by the Continental Congress as a monarch.[2]

Today, we might think of reliance on militias as a quaint notion tied to a time in history when wars could be seen coming for some

1 In fact, in the instance of Britain's provocation of the United States into the War of 1812, Madison hesitated and initially sought a declaration that Great Britain was in a state of war with the U.S. Congress eventually adopted a declaration of war against Great Britain. Beschloss (2018) goes on to argue that this set the precedent for presidential requests for war declarations and through Franklin Roosevelt would declare that a state of war already existed.

2 It is doubtful, given the disdain held by the Founders for the monarchy they had just broken away from that they would have agreed, necessarily, to such an arrangement. However, with growing frustration with the country's inability to move forward due to the shortcomings of the Articles of Confederation and the popularity of Washington it would not be hard to imagine a monarchy with Washington at its head.

time before their actual start. Nations could take the time to mobilize forces and perhaps even buy time for diplomacy to work before actual shooting took place. A similar concept has been used with regard to the so-called nuclear triad, where at least two parts of it could be recalled before full deployment (bombers and submarines). The contemporary descendant of the militias from colonial and revolutionary times is the National Guard, which remains under the civilian control of state governors and still takes time to call up into service. While the Guard is a backup force for the standing military, it also provides for defense against domestic insurrection and as a rescue and recovery force following natural disasters.

In *Federalist #24* Alexander Hamilton (1961b) made the case for a federal army and navy, to aid in both defense and commerce. In *Federalist #25* Hamilton argued that leaving the states to provide their own defense, under direction from the federal government, would be "oppressive to some States, dangerous to all, and baneful to the Confederacy"[3] (1961c). Hamilton went on to argue that the threat is common to all states, and therefore the defense should be common as well:

> The territories of Britain, Spain and of the Indian nations in our neighbourhood, do not border on particular States; but incircle the Union from Maine to Georgia. The danger, though in different degrees, is therefore common. And the means of guarding against it ought in like manner to be the objects of common councils and of a common treasury. It happens that some States, from local situation, are more directly exposed. New-York is of this class. Upon the plan of separate provisions, New-York would have to sustain the whole weight of the establishments requisite to her immediate safety, and to the mediate or ultimate protection of her neighbours. This would neither be equitable as it respected New-York, nor safe as it respected the other States.

Beyond the argument regarding the source of defense (national versus state, also known as the War Power), debate also centered around defining the War Power and limiting it. At the time there was, according to Adler and Gorman, a "prejudice" against standing armies; they

3 The reference to "the confederacy" here is to the organization of the government of the time under the Articles of Confederacy and not to the later constructed Confederate States of America.

report that six of the ratifying state conventions offered amendments to address the fact that "standing peacetime armies are "ever a menace to liberty"" (1975, 93). They contend that the Framers worked to counter that prejudice, arguing that it would be irrational to place limits on the power to provide for the common defense. At the same time, recognizing the power associated with a standing army, the Framers utilized the separation of powers and the system of checks and balances. For example, the President is the commander in chief, but the power to declare war lies with Congress, not the President.

The Framers argued that these checks and balances were a protection of liberty, but there were two issues that arose among many of the states that had to be addressed separately: the first was a general reluctance to surrender complete military power to the federal government, and the other was the ubiquitous belief that only an armed people can remain a free people. The first of those concerns was addressed in Article I, Section VIII of the Constitution, clauses 15 and 16 dealing with militias, while the second was addressed by the inclusion of the Second Amendment in the Bill of Rights.

Once again, we should emphasize that the use of the term "militia" in its historical context is far different from how it is often used today. The key difference comes from that wording alluded to earlier from the Second Amendment – "A well regulated Militia, being necessary to the security of a free State ..." – and refers to a government (state) sponsored organization for the purposes of common defense and response to insurrection[4] and other emergencies. This is not a reference to the contemporary use of the term, which is used as a label for voluntary

4 In Article I of The Constitution, Congress is given the power "To provide for calling forth the Militia to execute the Laws of the Union, suppress Insurrections and repel Invasions," but later legislation prohibited the use of the standing army to act as law enforcement except in very limited circumstances. State National Guard units, unless called into the service of the national government, can engage in law enforcement activity. This was one of the sticking points following Hurricane Katrina in Louisiana in 2005 when President George W. Bush wanted to federalize Louisiana's Guard, but the governor, Kathleen Blanco, refused. With her state and local police depleted by evacuations, she was relying on the National Guard to provide much needed law enforcement and if they were "called into service" they would no longer be able to do so.

organizations, not sponsored or controlled by the government and have no legal status and are often designed as a protest against what members see as an overbearing government.

Contemporary Applications of Militias (the National Guard)

The original conception of the militia, now the National Guard, kept under the control of the states, specifically their governors, was to have a ready reserve and a force that could respond rapidly to unrest like the Whiskey and Shay's Rebellions. The conception of the military evolved over time. Certainly, civilian control was still the central tenet, but we moved away from the militia-heavy military to a greater reliance on a standing force of some sort. As indicated earlier, the Constitution calls for an "army and a navy", and under the most literal interpretation would include only those services, yet we now have an air force (separated out from the Army at the end of World War II) and, most recently, a Space Force, expanding upon the Space Command within the Air Force.[5]

Typically, governors call up the National Guard to control civil protest or unrest, mostly to help control crowds and to provide a show of force or restore order after local law enforcement has been overwhelmed. At the same time, Guard units are summoned in response to natural disasters such as hurricanes, tornados, earthquakes, wildfires, and other weather-related catastrophes. Just before we began writing this section the Texas National Guard had been called up by Governor Gregg Abbott to help distribute food and water and to provide shelter after devastating winter storms and cold temperatures descended upon

5 There are now actually eight branches of the uniformed services of the United States, with the Marine Corps housed within the Department of the Navy and the Space Force housed within the Department of the Air Force. The eight branches are: the Army, the Navy, the Air Force, the Marine Corps, the Space Force, the Coast Guard (housed in the Department of Homeland Security, but can be transferred to the Department of the Navy during times of war), the United States Public Health Commissioned Corps, and the National Oceanic and Atmospheric Administration Commissioned Officer Corps.

the state. Just prior to that, we witnessed the confusion over calling up the Guard in the District of Columbia in response to the insurrection on January 6, 2021. In the District of Columbia, because it does not at this writing or at the time of the insurrection have the powers of a state, its Guard units are under the command of the Department of Defense. It has been reported that National Guard units did not arrive on the Capitol grounds until four or more hours after they were first requested by DC Metro Police. While at this writing, details of that day are still cloudy and investigations have just begun, there were reports that some of the reluctance to employ the Guard as a peremptory or preventative measure was due to concern over the optics of armed troops and razor wire protecting one the world's great symbols of democratic government.

While it was a tragic application of the concept, this concern is rooted in the very separation of the military from the government embodied by Washington's emulation of Cincinnatus and voluntarily stepping down from command of his troops. The debate over the appropriate use of the military in domestic settings is perhaps more a question of domestic tranquility than common defense. It was nonetheless an important discussion during the civil unrest in the summer of 2020 and in particular during the protests near the White House following the killing by Minneapolis police officers of George Floyd.[6]

To be sure, there are those in recent history who have bastardized the concept of the militia. All of our references thus far have been to what the Constitution, and many of the Framers referred to as "well-regulated" militias, those under the regulation of the various states. Many who fear the power of government, especially a centrally controlled one, have joined together to form what they call citizens' militias, but few, if any, would categorize these groups as militias in the constitutional sense. Ironically, the National Guard has been used to keep these contemporary iterations of militias under control.

Putting aside the place of the "militias" in our common defense, it is important to consider that even though the original language of the

6 At this writing, one officer has been charged with and convicted of murder and others have been charged with crimes related to Floyd's death.

Constitution appears somewhat limiting, Congress has used its implied powers and broader conception of providing for the common defense to evolve the military to suit the defense needs of the country over time. Providing for air power in both the army and navy, initially, and then separating the Army Air Corps out into the Air Force we know today and further distinguishing a Space Force from that Air Force is a reflection of the importance of the goal stated in the Preamble of providing for the common defense. To be sure, with a few bumps in the road the government has lived up to the goal and thus far no foreign enemy has been able to occupy geography in the United States for any substantial period of time and not at all since World War II.[7]

Bibliography

Adler, Mortimer Jerome, and William Gorman. 1975. *The American Testament.* New York: Praeger Publishers.

Beschloss, Michael. 2018. *Presidents of War: The Epic Story, from 1807 to Modern Times.* New York: Crown Publishing.

Hamilton, Alexander. 1961a. "Federalist #8." In *The Federalist. A Meridian Book,* edited by Jacob E. Cooke. New York: The World Publishing Company.

Hamilton, Alexander. 1961b. "Federalist #24." In *The Federalist. A Meridian Book,* edited by Jacob E. Cooke. New York: The World Publishing Company. .

Hamilton, Alexander. 1961c. "Federalist #25." In *The Federalist. A Meridian Book,* edited by Jacob E. Cooke. New York: The World Publishing Company.

Jay, John. 1961. "Federalist #3." In *The Federalist. A Meridian Book,* edited by Jacob E. Cooke. New York: The World Publishing Company.

Madison, James. 1961. "Federalist #41." In *The Federalist. A Meridian Book,* edited by Jacob E. Cooke. New York: The World Publishing Company.

Mason, George. 1776. "The Virginia Declaration of Rights." The National Archives, 2020 Accessed February 5, 2021, https://www.archives.gov/founding-docs/virginia-declaration-of-rights.

Ricks, Thomas E. 2020. *First Principles: What America's Founders Learned from the Greeks and Romans and How That Shaped Our Country.* New York: Harper Collins.

7 This statement should not be confused with the occupation of some "territories," particularly in the Pacific *during* WWII. Similarly, there are recent notable invasions of our cyberspace that were part of the basis of the investigation into Russian attempts to interfere in the elections in 2016 and 2020 as well as their recent attempts to conduct espionage against a number of government agencies and private entities.

Chapter Six

Promote the General Welfare

Among the objectives listed by the Framers, none is more heavily debated than the last two words of the title of this chapter. That phrase stems from the third article of the Articles of Confederation, and it occurs not only in the Preamble but again within the body of the Constitution, in the first paragraph of Article I, Section 8: "The Congress shall have Power To lay and collect Taxes, Duties, Imposts and Excises, to pay the Debts and provide for the common Defence and general Welfare of the United States." (National Archives 2020). Its meaning in the Articles of Confederation was unclear, and its use and meaning in the Constitution is repeatedly debated by politicians, academics and the judicial branch of the federal government.

General Welfare and the Size of Government

The main underlying issue of concern is the size of government. Given the "sweeping clause" that was placed at the end of Article I, Section 8 (that Congress shall have the power "to make all Laws which shall be necessary and proper for carrying into Execution the foregoing Powers, and all other Powers vested by this Constitution in the Government of the United States, or in any Department or Officer thereof"), the combined powers of taxing (and spending) and making laws can rightly lead many to be concerned with limiting those powers. Fear of such sweeping power being held by the government formed the basis of anti-federalist opposition to the new Constitution and led to the federalists compromising by adopting the Bill of Rights in the newly elected Congress.

This struggle was played out among the Framers as indicated in the writings of James Madison and Alexander Hamilton. In *Federalist #41* (originally published in January 1788) Madison (1961) opined that the language of Article I, Section 8 could be interpreted as "an unlimited commission to exercise every power which may be alleged to be necessary for the common defense or the general welfare" (1961). Madison feared that the power to tax and spend could be used for political purposes under the guise of the "general welfare." Alexander Hamilton, on the other hand, wrote in 1791 in support of that power:

> A Question has been made concerning the Constitutional right of the Government of the United States to apply this species of encouragement, but there is certainly no good foundation for such a question. The National Legislature has express authority "To lay and Collect taxes, duties, imposts and excises, to pay the debts and provide for the *Common defence* and *general welfare*" with no other qualifications than that "all duties, imposts and excises, shall be *uniform* throughout the United states, that no capitation or other direct tax shall be laid unless in proportion to numbers ascertained by a census or enumeration taken on the principles prescribed in the Constitution," and that "no tax or duty shall be laid on articles exported from any state." These three qualifications excepted, the power to *raise money* is *plenary*, and *indefinite;* and the objects to which it may be *appropriated* are no less comprehensive, than the payment of the public debts and the providing for the common defence and *"general Welfare."* The words *"general Welfare"* were doubtless intended to signify more than was expressed or imported in those which Preceded; otherwise numerous exigencies incident to the affairs of a Nation would have been left without a provision. The phrase is as comprehensive as any that could have been used; because it was not fit that the constitutional authority of the Union, to appropriate its revenues shou'd [*sic*]

> have been restricted within narrower limits than the "General Welfare" and because this necessarily embraces a vast variety of particulars, which are susceptible neither of specification nor of definition. (Hamilton 2020)

Whose Welfare?

While conservatives and liberals are likely to never agree on the benefits of small versus large government, an important point gets lost in that discussion. Professor Robert Reich, former Secretary of Labor under President Clinton, expressed this point quite effectively: "The size of government isn't the problem. That's a canard used to hide the far larger problem. The larger problem is that much of government is no longer working for the vast majority it's intended to serve. It's working instead for a small minority at the top" (2014). The forces of lobbyists and special interests have effectively captured Congress and work with them to support their own interests over those of Congress' constituents. This strategy, building for years, reached new heights during the Trump administration.

Welfare, in the context used in this discussion, is not as we would normally think of it – as what is often thought of as "government handouts" – but is more in the vein of creating an environment in which all people can flourish, whether economically, socially, or spiritually. Certainly, it can thus include such individual payments to assist the economically disadvantaged or those in temporary need. Often, the term "welfare" is used in a derogatory manner to refer to those who are seen as "lazy" or abusive of the generosity of the government and other citizens. This "stigma" is not what this discussion is about, at least not the vast majority of the discussion.

Contrary to the view of welfare (stigmatized or not) for individuals, in December of 2017 Congress passed a sweeping "tax reform" bill, the Tax Cuts and Jobs Act (TPC Staff 2017), which President Trump touted as being beneficial for working class Americans: "Our focus is on helping the folks who work in the mailrooms and the machine shops of America. The plumbers, the carpenters, the cops, the teachers, the truck drivers, the pipe-fitters, the people that like me best" (Horsley

2019). In fact the bill was a windfall for the wealthiest Americans, with over 60% of the benefit going to the top 20% of income earners, and for Corporate America, since the corporate tax rate was cut by 40%. Further evidence of Congress' focus on Corporations over constituents came in the form of the Liability Shield Bill that Republicans insisted on including in the COVID-19 Stimulus package (Iafolla 2020). The bill had a "safe harbor" provision that would immunize employers from lawsuits or enforcement actions related to the Coronavirus if they made good faith efforts to meet Government standards and guidance with regard to the virus. At the same time the Republican majority in the Senate moved to reduce the unemployment benefit being offered during a period of record high unemployment, much of which was related to the Coronavirus pandemic. The end result was a policy that clearly favored the wealthy and big business over the middle and working classes.

Collective or Individual Welfare?

Another issue with regard to the term "general welfare" that tends to split along party lines is the issue of whether the term refers to Americans in the collective or as individuals. Welch and Heilpern (2018) used the Corpus of Founding Era American English (COFEA) to analyze the frequency and use of the phrase "general welfare" in the documents entered into the COFEA collection. Their analysis concludes that the term is generally used to refer to the collective rather than the individual, although they admit that COFEA is not fool-proof. They also admit that some uses of the "mass-noun" refer to groups less than the totality of American citizens, "whether it be a country, army, society, or family … " (1074) These details lessen the impact of their conclusion.

C. Dean McGrath Jr. (2005), in his position as Deputy Assistant to President George H. W. Bush, used the Preamble to defend the administration's War on Terror, and he used a number of references to individual rights within the document. For example, he argues for the U. S. support for the elections in Afghanistan and Iraq "not for power or glory but because democracy and individual liberty and freedom are the right ('justice as fairness') outcome" (17).[1] He later states that "the concept of individual liberty has been a driving principle for our country's leaders since the Declaration of Independence and the Revolutionary War" (18).

McGrath also points out, with regard to the Preamble's reference to establishing justice, that "as numerous scholars have noted, justice is fundamentally a moral concept" (15). Morality is a concept measured and judged at the level of the individual. Further, in the section regarding providing for the common defense, McGrath recognizes that defense must be provided to individuals: "Since the earliest days of the Republic, the United States, like other countries, has used force and threatened the use of force to protect its citizens and its interests" (16). Citizens is not a collective term, but rather refers to a group of individuals (as opposed to citizenry). It is inconsistent to claim that our government has a responsibility to individual citizens for their liberty and justice, but not for their welfare.

Alexander Tsesis (2013), a constitutional scholar and former legislative advisor to Senator Edward Kennedy and the Judiciary Committee, takes a distinctly more liberal view:

> The core purpose of representative constitutionalism is the protection of individual rights for the general welfare. This maxim of governmental purpose for adjudication, regulation, and legislation is incorporated into the Declaration of independence and the Preamble to the Constitution. That ideal purpose of representative democracy is at the core of U. S. governance. It sets the directive for all three branches to legitimately exercise their respective powers. (1685)

Another Preamble, that to the Declaration of Independence, makes the case for individual rights in the words of Thomas Jefferson:

1 Clearly, McGrath is borrowing the wording from Rawls (1971, 2001). It is doubtful to us, however, that even with Rawls having volunteered for service during World War II, he became disillusioned with the military over the dropping of the atomic bomb on Hiroshima and the more personal experience of being ordered to discipline a fellow soldier and later considered the country's involvement in Vietnam to be un-American (King 2014).

> We hold these truths to be self-evident, that all men are created equal, that they are endowed by their Creator with certain unalienable Rights, that among these are Life, Liberty and the pursuit of Happiness.

Jefferson's words clearly indicate the individual nature of the rights the Founders and Framers were seeking to achieve for the American people. Life occurs en masse but is experienced individually; the same with liberty. Happiness is a feeling experienced by individuals.

Common Good or General Welfare?

The "common good" so often promoted by the Founders and Framers recognized the community's responsibility to its individual citizens. That same sense of common good was the basis for the Civil Rights movement; until the Civil Rights Act was passed in 1964, Black Americans were not considered to be created equal, and their rights were suppressed by their government. In response to a public statement of concern by eight White religious leaders of the south, Dr. Martin Luther King Jr. wrote of the mutual suffering among Black Americans in Alabama and Georgia:

> I am cognizant of the interrelatedness of all communities and states. I cannot sit idly by in Atlanta and not be concerned about what happens in Birmingham. Injustice anywhere is a threat to justice everywhere. We are caught in an inescapable network of mutuality, tied in a single garment of destiny. Whatever affects one directly affects all indirectly. (1963)

The Framers made sufficient mention of the "common good" and individual rights that it would seem contrary to claim that the federal government has an individual duty to provide every American with justice, defense, and liberty, but they are not responsible for individual welfare. But even if we assume that the government is responsible for providing a "common" level of welfare rather than an "individual" level, it is reasonable to assume that they are responsible for a minimum level of welfare at the individual level. One major difference between the two parties is with where that minimum lies.

We would be remiss not to mention that much of what is meant by common good or general welfare falls within what are commonly considered the reserved powers. These are the powers reserved by the 10th Amendment to the states. The 10th Amendment reads: "The powers not delegated to the United States by the Constitution, nor prohibited by it to the States, are reserved to the States respectively, or to the people." Typically, this includes policy areas like land use, other property laws, criminal codes, marriage and divorce laws, other family law, the administration of health and safety rules and programs, professional licensing, and more. All of this falls under what is known as the police power. Certainly, not all general welfare policy lies solely with the states, but much is still within the purview of the national government. If the national government had no role in providing for the general welfare and all of that responsibility fell exclusively to the states, why would the Framers give it such a prominent role by mentioning it in the Preamble itself?

General Welfare as Economic Rights

It is reasonable to conclude that a government, particularly a national one, that collects taxes on an individual basis has a responsibility to those individuals to see to their minimum basic needs; food, shelter, and clothing. It is not unreasonable, therefore, to conclude that able-bodied people should be supplied with the opportunity to perform meaningful work and to provide more than a bare subsistence for their families. If half of the people are wealthy and the other half are poor, then on average the group has sufficient resources, but there will be little chance of domestic tranquility. President Franklin Delano Roosevelt stated as much in his January 1944 State of the Union address, also known as the Second Bill of Rights speech:

> It is our duty now to begin to lay the plans and determine the strategy for the winning of a lasting peace and the establishment of an American standard of living higher than ever before known. We cannot be content, no matter how high that general standard of living may be, if some fraction of

> our people—whether it be one-third or one-fifth or one-tenth- is ill-fed, ill-clothed, ill housed, and insecure. This Republic had its beginning, and grew to its present strength, under the protection of certain inalienable political rights—among them the right of free speech, free press, free worship, trial by jury, freedom from unreasonable searches and seizures. They were our rights to life and liberty. As our Nation has grown in size and stature, however—as our industrial economy expanded—these political rights proved inadequate to assure us equality in the pursuit of happiness. We have come to a clear realization of the fact that true individual freedom cannot exist without economic security and independence. "Necessitous men are not free men." People who are hungry and out of a job are the stuff of which dictatorships are made. (1944)

President Roosevelt fully promoted individual welfare in his speech, and placed the responsibility for making his Economic Bill of Rights happen squarely on the backs of Congress, "for it is definitely the responsibility of the Congress to do so" (1944). Three Supreme Court cases that took place during the Great Depression served as support for his position. In *The United States v. Butler* (1936), a case involving farm subsidies, Justice Owen Roberts summarized the issue and the court's opinion on the issue of the general welfare quite effectively:

> Since the foundation of the nation, sharp differences of opinion have persisted as to the true interpretation of the phrase. Madison asserted it amounted to no more than a reference to the other powers enumerated in the subsequent clauses of the same section; that, as the United States is a government of limited and enumerated powers, the grant of power to tax and spend for the general national welfare must be confined to the enumerated legislative fields committed to the Congress. ... Hamilton, on the other hand, maintained the clause confers a power separate and distinct from those later enumerated is not restricted in meaning by the grant of them, and Congress consequently has a substantive power to tax and to appropriate, limited only by the requirement that it shall be exercised to provide for the general welfare of the United States. ... Mr. Justice Story, in his Commentaries, espouses the Hamiltonian position. ... Study of all these leads us to conclude that the reading advocated by Mr. Justice Story is the correct one. While, therefore, the power to tax is not unlimited, its confines are set in the clause which confers it, and not in those of section 8 which bestow and define the legislative powers of the Congress. It results that the power of Congress to authorize

expenditure of public moneys for public purposes is not limited by the direct grants of legislative power found in the Constitution. (41)

In 1937 The Supreme Court decided a pair of cases that dealt with the Social Security Act, in which both opinions were written by Justice Cardozo. In *Steward Machine Co. v. Davis* Justice Cardozo cited *U. S. v. Butler* in his opinion to support the use of general revenue funds for assisting states in administering their unemployment compensation laws:

> During the years 1929 to 1936, when the country was passing through a cyclical depression, the number of the unemployed mounted to unprecedented heights. ... Disaster to the breadwinner meant disaster to dependents. Accordingly the roll of the unemployed, itself formidable enough, was only a partial roll of the destitute or needy. The fact developed quickly that the states were unable to give the requisite relief. The problem had become national in area and dimensions. There was need of help from the nation if the people were not to starve. It is too late today for the argument to be heard with tolerance that in a crisis so extreme the use of the moneys of the nation to relieve the unemployed and their dependents is a use for any purpose narrower than the promotion of the general welfare. (20)

Cardozo's words seem quite appropriate for the circumstances the United States faced during the pandemic of 2020. Also in 1937, Justice Cardozo wrote the opinion in *Helvering v. Davis,* where arguments surrounded the old age pension provisions of the Social Security Act. Once again Cardozo recognized the need for federal assistance at the individual level during difficult times:

> The purge of nation-wide calamity that began in 1929 has taught us many lessons. Not the least is the solidarity of interests that may once have seemed to be divided. ... Spreading from state to state, unemployment is an ill not particular but general, which may be checked, if Congress so determines, by the resources of the nation. If this can have been doubtful until now, our ruling today in the case of the Steward Machine Co., supra, has set the doubt at rest. But the ill is all one or at least not greatly different whether men are thrown out of work because there is no longer work to do or because the disabilities of age make them incapable of doing it. Rescue becomes necessary irrespective of the cause.

President Roosevelt's Bill of Economic Rights found its inspiration in Jefferson's Preamble to the Declaration of Independence, and gained strength from the Supreme Court decisions in *Butler, Steward, Helvering* and others. His speech did not refer to the phrase general welfare; instead he insisted that "after this war is won we must be prepared to move forward, in the implementation of these rights, to new goals of human happiness and well-being" (1944). Happiness and well-being are individual concepts.

Adler and Gorman (1975) refer to Roosevelt's use of the term "economic" in his Bill of Economic Rights as "broad," claiming that while he did indeed want to promote the general welfare, Hamilton intended to do so by assisting in the growth of businesses.

> All governmental actions in aid of "the economy," to fight inflation or recession, would be as much exercises of the welfare power as measures of assistance to the seriously indigent, the debilitated old, the helplessly sick or disabled, and those whom we have the habit of speaking of as "on welfare." Roosevelt's very broad use of the term "economic" includes such things as the right to a decent home, the right to adequate medical care, the right to sufficient schooling, as well as the rights of every farmer and every businessman. Used thus broadly, the term encompasses all the external conditions which can be judged indispensable to leading a decent human life. (1975, 107–8)

While without question the assistance given to businesses to aid in growth is part of promoting the general welfare, it is not enough – certainly it is not enough for the "seriously indigent, the debilitated old, the helplessly sick or disabled." Any and all efforts to provide for the general welfare should be able to be tied directly back to the impact they have on people, on families or communities, or they are not serving the interest of their constituents. Adler and Gorman make this point effectively:

> The whole of Roosevelt's State of the Union Address in 1944 charges Congress with the task of doing distributive justice. To assure to all "equality in the pursuit of happiness" is a work of justice. All human beings, equally in possession of the inherent human right to pursue happiness, can rightfully expect from the political society of which they are members and from the government of which they are together constituents, proportionately

> equitable support in their exercise of that right. Justice *requires* government to promote the general welfare, understood as an equitable participation by all in the economic or other external goods which are judged indispensable to the pursuit of happiness. All human beings should have an equal opportunity to fare well in that pursuit. (1975 108–9- emphasis added)

For consideration of the general welfare, the Preamble provides more than a simple rhetorical goal. If Adler and Gorman are correct, the Preamble *demands* that the government, both national and state, strive to provide that welfare – that common good. True, there may be limits via Supreme Court interpretation and the 10th Amendment to what the national government may do, but Article I, Section Eight, of the Constitution provides fertile ground to be tilled.

Bibliography

Adler, Mortimer Jerome, and William Gorman. 1975. *The American Testament.* New York: Praeger Publishers.

Charles C. Steward Machine Co. v. Davis, 301 U. S. 548 (1937).

Hamilton, Alexander. 2020. "Alexander Hamilton's Final Version of the Report on the Subject of Manufactures." The National Archives. Accessed February 10, 2021, https://www.archives.gov/founding-docs/constitution.

Helvering, Commissioner of Internal Revenue, et al. v. Davis, 301 U. S. 619 (1937).

Horsley, Scott. 2019. "After 2 Years, Trump Tax Cuts Have Failed To Deliver On GOP's Promises." Npr.org. Accessed February 12, 2021, https://www.npr.org/2019/12/20/789540931/2-years-later-trump-tax-cuts-have-failed-to-deliver-on-gops-promises.

Iafolla, Robert. 2020. "Employers Get Major Protections in GOP Liability Shield Bill." Bloomberglaw.com. Accessed February 12, 2021, https://news.bloomberglaw.com/daily-labor-report/employers-get-major-protections-in-gop-liability-shield-bill.

Jefferson, Thomas. 1776. "The Declaration of Independence." National Archives. Accessed February 28, 2021, https://www.archives.gov/founding-docs/declaration-transcript.

King, Iain. 2014. "Thinker at War: Rawls." *Military History Monthly,* June 13. Accessed February 26, 2021, https://www.military-history.org/articles/thinkers-at-war-john-rawls.htm.

King Jr., Dr. Martin Luther. 1963. "Letter From Birmingham Jail." Csuchico.edu. Accessed February 12, 2021, https://www.csuchico.edu/iege/_assets/documents/susi-letter-from-birmingham-jail.pdf.

Madison, James. 1961. "Federalist #41." In *The Federalist. A Meridian Book,* edited by Jacob E. Cooke. New York: The World Publishing Company.

McGrath Jr., C. Dean. 2005. "The Genius of the Constitution: The Preamble and the War on Terror." *Georgetown Journal of Law and Public Policy* 13: 13–19.

National Archives, The. 2020. "The Constitution of the United States." Archives.gov. Accessed June 18, 2020, https://www.archives.gov/founding-docs/constitution.

Rawls, John. 1971. *A Theory of Justice* (Original edition). Cambridge: Belknap Press of Harvard University Press.

Rawls, John. 2001. *Justice as Fairness: A Restatement*, 2nd ed. Cambridge: Harvard University Press.

Reich, Robert. 2014, December 24. "It's Not the Size of the Government That's the Problem." *Baltimore Sun*. Retrieved, https://www.baltimoresun.com/opinion/op-ed/bs-ed-reich-government-20141224-story.html.

Roosevelt, Franklin. 1944. "State of the Union Message to Congress." Fdrlibrary.marist.edu. Accessed February 14, 2021, http://www.fdrlibrary.marist.edu/archives/address_text.html.

TPC Staff. 2017. "Distributional Analysis of the Conference Agreement for the Tax Cuts and Jobs Act." Tax Policy Center, Urban Institute & Brookings Institution. Accessed February 25, 2021, https://www.taxpolicycenter.org/publications/distributional-analysis-conference-agreement-tax-cuts-and-jobs-act/full

Tsesis, Alexander. 2013. "Maxim Constitutionalism: Liberal Equality for the Common Good." *Texas Law Review* 91: 1609–85.

United States v. Butler, 297 U. S. 1 (1936).

Welch, John, and James Heilpern. "Recovering our Forgotten Preamble." *Southern California Law Review* 91: 1021–38.

Chapter Seven

Secure the Blessings of Liberty to Ourselves and Our Posterity

From the start, Americans have been lovers of liberty. The independence of spirit that is required to cut all ties with home and start a new life elsewhere are still highly valued today. Liberty, however, may be curtailed or denied in a representative government. Adler and Gorman (1975) quote Charles H. McIlwain, from *Constitutionalism: Ancient and Modern* (1940): "The two fundamental correlative elements of constitutionalism for which all lovers of liberty must yet fight are the legal limits to arbitrary power and a complete political responsibility of government to the governed" (109). But as the Framers well knew, power conceived in liberty but conferred upon representatives can lead to abuses of power. James Madison (1961) warned as much in *Federalist #51*:

> If men were angels, no government would be necessary. If angels were to govern men, neither external nor internal controls on government would be necessary. In framing a government which is to be by men over men, the great difficulty lies in this: you must first enable the government to control the governed; and in the next place oblige it to control itself. A dependence on the people is, no doubt, a primary control on the government; but experience has taught mankind the necessity of auxiliary precautions.

This understanding motivated the Framers to place legal limits on the powers granted to the elected representatives, to separate those powers among the three branches of the new government, and to build in checks and balances designed to limit abuses of power. In addition, a number of individual rights are guaranteed in the body of the Constitution. For example, suspension of the writ of habeas corpus is limited to cases of rebellion or invasion, and federal or state bills of attainder are prohibited. When the original document (the part prior to the adoption of the first ten amendments) was presented to the American people, many who were even more leary of central power than the Framers themselves, they expressed their fears in pamphlets designed to counter the pro-Constitution arguments of the Framers. With the presentation of their arguments these concerned patriots created our earliest partisan divide, that between the Federalists (who supported ratification) and the Anti-Federalists (who opposed ratification). The Anti-Federalists made clear that they were concerned that the habeas corpus and contract protections were not sufficient safeguards of individual liberties. Though the Federalists won the ratification debate and sufficient votes in the states to gain ratification, further protections were written into the Bill of Rights as a response to the concerns expressed in the state ratifying conventions. This recognition of individual liberties has continued through the 20th century, resulting in the 13th, 14th, 15th, 19th, 24th and 26th amendments.

Limits on Government Power

All of these efforts were designed to address the first of McIlwain's "two fundamental correlative elements," arbitrary power. The second element is most famously summed up by President Lincoln in his Emancipation Proclamation: government of the people, by the people and for the people, or self-governing. The audaciousness of the American experiment lies in the idea of its being a self-ruling nation. Complications arise, however, from the relationship between the representatives and their constituents.

The disciplines of both authors – Political Science and Finance respectively – refer to this as an Agency issue or principal-agent models; the managers of a firm (our representatives) act as agents for the common shareholders (us, their constituents) and make decisions (vote) on their (our) behalf.[1] However, agents have the opportunity to consume perquisites (take advantage of their positions of power) that benefit themselves (or their party) at the expense of the owners (us, their constituents). Firms are therefore forced to make efforts to align their agents' behavior with their own goals in order to minimize such abuses. Parshall and Twombly (2020) have summarized the application of principal-agent models to the control of bureaucratic behavior. They note the work of political scientist Terry Moe, who characterized "politics ... [as] structured by a chain of principal-agent relationships" (Moe 1985, 764–65). Similarly, we, the people, must make efforts to curb abuses of power by our elected representatives. Parshall and Twombly put it this way: "The basis of the model is that the ultimate principals in a democratic form of government are the citizens who exercise their option to renew the contract through the mechanism of the ballot" (2020, 55).

Breakin' Up Is Not So Hard to Do

Conservatives often refer to more laws as "big government," and they blame big government for restricting economic growth. In doing so they ignore the fact that laws and regulations are put in place for a purpose, many times to prevent conditions that are unsafe for workers, or that grant some entities an unfair advantage over their competitors. The Occupational Safety and Health Administration (OSHA) is

1 Commonly, this issue is represented in Political Science as deriving from the understanding of government gained via social contract theory and in business or Finance as deriving from the Theory of the Firm. In the disciplines of Business, Economics, and Finance the roots of this literature derive from theories of the firm (see e.g., Alchian and Demsetz 1972, Fama 1980). In Political Science many have applied theories of the firm and principal-agent models, especially to control of both bureaucrats and elected officials (see e.g., Heclo 1975, 1977, Nathan 1975, 1983, Brehm and Gates 1997, Lewis 2008, 2009).

the governmental agency that oversees safety at workplaces, to prevent accidents whenever they can, and to hold employers accountable for the results when they can't. While employers dislike the OSHA regulations, the labor force overwhelmingly appreciates having them around keeping everyone honest. OSHA owes its existence to the influence of organized labor in the political process, particularly in the 1960s. Antitrust laws exist to prevent monopolies, because competition is good for consumers, not for industry. The 1970s saw two of the largest antitrust suits filed to date: in 1974 the Department of Justice (DOJ) filed an antitrust suit against American Telephone and Telegraph (AT&T), which led to their divestiture in 1984, and in 1975 the DOJ filed a similar suit against International Business Machines (IBM), the result of a 1969 antitrust suit filed by the Southern District of New York. That case was withdrawn for lacking merit. Microsoft spent most of the 1990s fighting antitrust charges in and out of court. Interestingly, the two cases were settled on the same day – January 8, 1982 – but with the AT&T case having a much greater impact on the structure and size of the company going forward. Within two years AT&T would be out of the local telephone business and provide the more lucrative long distance service. Both suits were in some ways racing against potential congressional action that might have been more harsh than the settlements. While AT&T had been moving steadily into the personal computer market, IBM had been buying up parts of a long distance carrier and a communications manufacturer. Perhaps regulators hoped the new competition between the two tech giants would provide its own regulation.[2]

Even in the 21st century corporations like Microsoft and Google spend time and resources fighting antitrust laws in order to maintain an advantage that their competitors cannot overcome. Such advantages work for the firm but against competitors and the consumer, so not only consumers but also small businesses appreciate that the Department of Justice enforces antitrust laws.

2 Steve Coll's *The Deal of the Century: The Breakup of AT&T* is a detailed narrative of the AT&T antitrust suit with periodic references to the IBM case as well.

John Locke makes this point effectively in Chapter Seven of his Second Treatise on Civil Government, aptly titled Of Paternal Power (1821):

> For law, in its true notion, is not so much the limitation as the direction of a free and intelligent agent to his proper interest, and prescribes no farther than is for the general good of those under the law. Could they be happier without it, the law, as a useless thing, would of itself vanish; and that ill deserves the name of confinement which hedges us in only from bogs and precipices. So that however it may be mistaken, the end of the law is not to abolish or restrain, but to preserve and enlarge freedom. For in all the states of created beings, where there is no law there is no freedom. For liberty is to be free from restraint and violence from others, which cannot be where there is no law; and is not, as we are told, "a liberty for every man to do what he lists." For who could be free, when every other man's humour might domineer over him? But a liberty to dispose and order freely as he lists his person, actions, possessions, and his whole property within the allowance of those laws under which he is, and therein not to be subject to the arbitrary will of another, but freely follow his own. (234)

Locke argues that laws offer freedom, not limitation, for the general public. Antitrust laws prevent monopolies, and so they promote competition and support small business. Consumer Protection laws are designed to protect consumers against such things as a poor quality or unsafe product. Adler and Gorman (1975) agree:

> It is worth recording that there is no body of texts in the founding literature which urges that the sphere of unregulated conduct should be very large, or as large as possible. That literature, in other words, does not espouse the position later to be called "minimalism" – the view that that government governs best which governs least, because it thereby enlarges the sphere of personal liberty. (117)

In addition to Locke, Adler and Gorman use the lectures of James Wilson (originally published in 1790) to support their position that personal liberty (or as Wilson refers to it, natural liberty) is "preserved or enlarged" by regulation:

> Nature has implanted in man the desire of his own happiness; she has inspired him with many tender affections towards others, especially in the

> near relations of life; she has endowed him with intellectual and with active powers; she has furnished him with a natural impulse to exercise his powers for his own happiness, and the happiness of those for whom he entertains such tender affections. If all this be true, the undeniable consequence is, that he has a right to exert those powers for the accomplishment of those purposes, in such a manner, and upon such objects, as his inclination and judgment shall direct; provided he does no injury to others; and provided some publick [sic] interests do not demand his labours. This right is natural liberty. (Wilson 2007, 1056)

This argument, to Adler and Gorman (1975) "not only confirms Locke's doctrine, but also argues, by implication at least, that that government governs best which governs, not least or most, but most justly; and that human beings have as much personal liberty as they deserve, or can use justly, when their conduct is regulated by just laws" (117). It is not the number of laws that is the issue, but rather the just or unjust nature of laws that matters.

Laws and Liberty

Laws and regulations do not magically appear; they are put on the books for a reason. If that reason becomes irrelevant over time then the law deserves to be taken off the books. However, removing laws and regulations without addressing the underlying reasons they were originally put in place is short-sighted and irresponsible, and the unsafe or unfair behaviors those laws were meant to prevent will return. Laws and regulations are not big government, they are the government watching out for its constituency. After all, our representatives are elected by the voters, not by industry.

In this regard, we cannot improve upon the final paragraph from Adler and Gorman's treatise on the Preamble:

> The title page of the first published edition of James Wilson's *Works* contained a motto from Cicero: Lex fundamentum est libertatis, qua fruimur. Legum omnes servi sumus, ut liberi esse possimus. "Law is the foundation of the liberty we enjoy. We are all servants of the laws in order that we can be free." (1975, 118)

It is important to appreciate that McIlwain's two correlative elements are *political* liberties; crucial in theory, but simply not in the line of sight for many Americans on a daily basis. Instead governments tend to be judged by their handling of *personal* liberties. Indeed, Adler and Gorman (1975) opine that personal liberty is more fundamental than political liberty, as it is "grounded in law, in the sense of being "secured" by the law and government." (115) Within that opinion they argue that the Framers were in agreement as to the relation between law and liberty:

> How would such personal liberty have been defined by the American founding leaders? In the context of the Declaration of Independence, personal liberty would consist in the capacity to exercise effectively the natural right equally possessed by all men to the pursuit of happiness. Was government necessary for conferring such liberty on citizens and safeguarding it? The answer was firmly in the affirmative. Are not laws antithetical to such liberty, so that the more law, the less liberty? The answer was firmly in the negative. (115–6)

This last point belies a basic tenet of contemporary Conservative thought: that laws and regulations restrict freedom and therefore need to be culled. According to Adler and Gorman, the Framers were in total agreement on this, as they were all familiar with John Locke's tome *Second Treatise on Civil Government*. "There is no evidence anywhere that there was any fundamental disagreement with his "resolution" of age-old questions about the relation between law and liberty." (Adler and Gorman 1975, 116)

Individual Liberties

Adler and Gorman (1975) recommend extending the term "Bill of Rights" to include more than simply the first 10 amendments:

> … – those that abolish slavery; declare all persons born or naturalized in the United States subject to its jurisdiction as citizens thereof; forbid the states to abridge the privileges or immunities of citizens of the United States, to deprive any person of life, liberty or property without due process of law, or

> to deny to any person the equal protections of the laws; prohibit the denial or abridgement of voting rights because of race, sex, or failure to pay poll taxes.
>
> By such an extended Bill of Rights, taken together with the results of the separation of powers and of checks and balances, Americans placed constitutional limits on arbitrary power. These constitutional limitations intended to provide basic security for one freedom, fundamental throughout the revolutionary era – freedom *from* arbitrary power. (111)

The concept can be viewed in the context of the process of the selective incorporation of the Bill of Rights under the aegis of the 14th Amendment. This is the process by which the courts have, on a case by case basis, used the 14th Amendment to force states to follow the same protections of individual freedom as the national government must.

The Bill of Rights, and its extensions, is the mechanism by which we have attempted to "secure the blessings of liberty to ourselves and our posterity." Certainly, measures like the various incarnations of the Civil Rights Act, particularly the 1964 version, and the Voting Rights Act of 1965 have helped us achieve the goal. However, those are mere laws, laws that can be easily changed at the whim of a majority in the legislative branch (in cooperation with a similarly minded-executive). It is the Bill of Rights and the amendments that extended them, by adding liberties and by expanding the categories of people covered by them, that truly secure our liberty. While "mere laws" can be overturned by simple majorities, constitutional amendments are by definition and design hard to overturn.

Volume after volume has been written about the wonders of the Bill of Rights and its protections of basic freedoms – speech, press, religion, association, trial by jury, protection from unreasonable search and seizure, and so on – and we cannot address them fully in this venue. Instead, we would like to note that they have been extended or expanded.

Bibliography

Adler, Mortimer Jerome, and William Gorman. 1975. *The American Testament*. New York: Praeger Publishing.

Alchian, Armen A., and Harold Demsetz. 1972. "Production, Information Costs, and Economic Organization." *American Economic Review* 62(5): 777–95.

Brehm, John, and Scott Gates. 1997. *Working, Shirking, and Sabotage: Bureaucratic Response to a Democratic Public.* Ann Arbor: University of Michigan Press.

Coll, Steve. 1986. *The Deal of the Century: The Breakup of AT&T.* New York: Atheneum.

Fama, Eugene. 1980. "Agency Problems and the Theory of the Firm." *Journal of Political Economy* 88(2): 288–307.

Heclo, Hugh. 1975. "OMB and the Presidency – The Problem of 'Neutral Competence'." *The Public Interest* 38 (Winter): 80–98.

Heclo, Hugh. 1977. *A Government of Strangers: Executive Politics in Washington.* Washington, DC: Brookings.

Lewis, David E. 2008. *The Politics of Presidential Appointments: Political Control and Bureaucratic Performance.* Princeton, NJ: Princeton University Press.

Lewis, David E. 2009. "Revisiting the Administrative residency: Policy, Patronage, and Agency Competence." *Presidential Studies Quarterly* 39(1): 60–73.

Locke, John. 1821. *Second Treatise on Civil Government.* London: Whitmore and Feng.

Madison, James. 1961. "Federalist #51." In *The Federalist. A Meridian Book,* edited by Jacob E. Cooke. New York: The World Publishing Company.

McIlwain, Charles Howard. 1940. *Constitutionalism: Ancient and Modern.* Ithaca, NY: Cornell University Press.

Moe, Terry. 1985. "The Politicized Presidency." In *The New Direction in American Politics,* edited by John E. Chubb and Paul E. Peterson, 235–71. Washington, DC: Brookings Institution.

Nathan, Richard P. 1975. *The Plot That Failed: Nixon and the Administrative Presidency.* New York: John Wiley & Sons.

Nathan, Richard P. 1983. *The Administrative Presidency.* New York: John Wiley & Sons.

Parshall, Lisa K., and Jim Twombly. 2020. *Directing the Whirlwind: The Trump Presidency and the Deconstruction of the Administrative State.* New York: Peter Lang Publishing, Inc.

Wilson, James. 2007. *The Collected Works of James Wilson,* edited by Kermit L. Hall and Mark David Hall, vol. 2. Indianapolis. IN: Liberty Fund.

Chapter Eight

A Perfectible Union

Still Seeking Justice, Domestic Tranquility, a Common Defense, General Welfare, and the Blessings of Liberty

We noted earlier that human beings, at least in the eyes of Rousseau are not perfect, but are perfectible. We suggest that our Union may not, nor perhaps ever, be perfect, but it is *perfectible*. It is not our perfection that the Preamble seeks, but its words – "a *more perfect* union" (emphasis added) – serve as a measure of what can be, what we should be, and what we must seek to do; even if we stumble on that path.

In the previous chapters, we have looked at how history and public policy measure up to the goals set forth by the Framers in the Preamble to the Constitution. We have seen how we have grown as a Union, first in terms of our size and economic prowess, and then through our pursuit of the other five goals. It was hard in 2020, with social and racial unrest, a failed attempt to lawfully remove a sitting president, a raging pandemic, and an economy as much on life support as so many of our fellow citizens who had fallen victim to COVID-19, to feel that we are anywhere near the Rousseauvian perfectibility suggested by that simple phrase: "a more perfect union." There is, however, hope.

Chapter Recaps

In Chapter One we laid out what the Preamble is and how the Framers might have viewed it. We also defined several ways in which the Constitution can and has been interpreted by scholars and Supreme Court justices alike. While taking the view that the Constitution is a living document, we recognized the value of understanding the original meaning or intent as a starting point. Since our subject matter was the Preamble and its larger goals and not the finer points of the more weighty portions of the document, it is in some ways more important to begin with what the words mean. This established a baseline for our analysis to come in the subsequent chapters.

Our case began with a discussion of what the Framers likely meant by "a more perfect union" in Chapter Two. In this discussion, we placed the goals of the Preamble in the context of periods of internal national conflict, particularly conflict that could be traced back to certain compromises made by the Framers in order to establish a government that would be at least minimally acceptable to all 13 states. The Civil War, Manifest Destiny, the American Industrial Revolution, the Great Depression, and more recent partisan polarization – including the insurrection on January 6, 2021 that was an attempt by supporters of President Trump to stop the certification of the Electoral College votes from the states – are the lenses through which we view the striving toward perfection of our Union.

We provided a working definition of "justice" in Chapter Three and through discussion of events in history and more recent times we once again applied the notion that we have not been and are not perfect. However, we argued that through conscious corrections of earlier mistakes we, as a nation, once again demonstrate our collective perfectibility.

In Chapter Four, we addressed the issue of civil peace and noted its ties to the establishment of justice. We examined the balance between public safety and personal liberty. We made note of the old adage from Ben Franklin that those who would sacrifice liberty for the sake of security deserve neither.[1] We examined the efforts of various, particularly more recent, administrations to handle that balance.

1 The actual quote is: "Those who would give up essential Liberty, to purchase a little temporary Safety, deserve neither Liberty nor Safety."

Our discussion in Chapter Five touched upon the delicate balance of power between the federal government and the states, especially with respect to providing a common defense. The oaths federal officers take include a promise to defend the Constitution against all enemies, foreign and domestic. Yet, as we noted, it is the defense against foreign enemies that is perhaps the "essential object" of any central government.[2]

We endeavored, in Chapter Six to address how the framers intended the "general welfare" to be promoted. In spite of the modern stigma associated with welfare and its more narrow meaning – the provision of public payments to the underprivileged in society – we also took a broader view of the concept and looked at it through the lens of recent events and the responses to them by recent administrations and congresses.

The Bill of Rights, we noted in Chapter Seven, though flawed, is the single best assurance of the "blessings of liberty." We had noted earlier as well that with no Bill of Rights included in the original document put forth to the states for ratification, the Preamble was to serve as the intention of the Framers as to the limits and extent of the powers of government. Without taking the same volume, and admittedly depth, as other texts on the protection of civil rights and liberties we laid out an abbreviated case for the Bill of Rights and other amendments to the Constitution providing for the furtherance of the blessings of liberty *and* the perfection of the Union.

The Preamble and Pop Culture

Nor should we ignore the relevance of the Preamble to popular culture. The sweeping script is easily recognizable whether under the protective glass at the National Archives in Washington, DC or in replications of the document in books or as art. The first three words – "We the People" – adorn poems, speeches, and textbooks. For example, a Google search for "We the People book" returned 5.2 billion results.[3] Naturally,

2 Certainly, recent events in the United States have moved domestic enemies to a place of central concern, particularly for federal law enforcement agencies.

3 As of January 31, 2021.

many of those results involve the titles for textbooks at the college and K-12 levels of education. Other results included children's coloring books, graphic novels, collections of art, and so on. A similar search for "We the People song" returned 239,000 results.[4] The Preamble has made it into a production of Schoolhouse Rock Live by the Dallas Children's Theater, including an animated version that quite reasonably replicates the feel of the original Schoolhouse Rock videos.

One striking appearance of those three words, and those that followed, is easily remembered by science fiction fans in an episode of the original *Star Trek* television series (Season Two, Episode 23). The crew of *The Enterprise* travels to a planet with a vaguely familiar disagreement over philosophical differences between races or nations of people – the Yangs and the Kohms.[5] Throughout the episode the leader of the Yangs references what appears to be some mystical document with equally mystical words. As the plot nears conclusion, Captain Kirk suddenly realizes that he recognizes the slurred and poorly pronounced "E'ed plebnista" as "We the People of the United States." Kirk launches into a fiery reading and defense of the importance of the words:

> **KIRK:** I did not recognise those words, you said them so badly, Without meaning.
>
> **ELDER:** No! No! Only the eyes of a chief may see the Ee'd Plebnista.
>
> **KIRK:** This was not written for chiefs. (general consternation) Hear me! Hear this! Among my people, we carry many such words as this from many lands, many worlds. Many are equally good and are as well respected, but wherever we have gone, no words have said this thing of importance in quite this way. Look at these three words written larger than the rest, with a special pride never written before or since. Tall words proudly saying We the People. That which you call Ee'd Plebnista was not written for the chiefs or the kings or the warriors or the rich and powerful, but for all the people! Down the centuries, you have slurred the meaning of the words, 'We, the people of the United States, in order to form a more perfect union, establish

4 A slight change in the search parameter by leaving the quotation marks only around "We the People" and song outside of the quote yielded over 6 million results.

5 An obvious reference to Yankees and Communists, especially with Kohms seemingly Asian in appearance (no doubt a reference to the Communist China of the 1960s, the time of *Star Trek*'s run on TV), and the ideological differences between a democratic country and one governed by an authoritarian regime.

justice, ensure domestic tranquillity, provide for the common defence, promote the general welfare, and secure the blessings of liberty to ourselves and our posterity, do ordain and establish this constitution.' These words and the words that follow were not written only for the Yangs, but for the Kohms as well!

CLOUD: The Kohms?

KIRK: They must apply to everyone or they mean nothing! Do you understand?

CLOUD: I do not fully understand, one named Kirk. But the holy words will be obeyed. I swear it.

It is worthy of note that the reading of the Preamble in this episode is done by the actor William Shatner, perhaps best known for his often melodramatic portrayal of Captain Kirk, who originates from Canada. The reading by a non-American only goes to make the larger point regarding the impact the Preamble has, especially those most important first three words: We the People.

The Preamble as Policy

How do we, the people, help to achieve a more perfect union? What can we do to pursue the changes we seek from our government? It is not simply to vote – voting is the *last* step in the process. Howard Dean, one-time presidential candidate, elected governor of Vermont five times, and former Democratic National Committee Chair, wrote "In my mind, voting gets you a D. If you want to live in a healthy democracy. If you want an A, you have to vote. *And* you have to work in a campaign … . To get an A+ you have to run for office yourself" (2004, 186). Of course we must seek and vet representatives whom we believe will represent us accurately and fairly once in office. These things are given. What more is required?

We can use the Preamble as a checklist of the general nature of the policies and legislation to be promoted by our representatives. We can require of our representatives that they explain in specific detail how the policies and legislation they intend to pursue will help to:

- Establish justice;
- Insure domestic tranquility;
- Provide for the common defense;

- Promote the general welfare;
- Secure the blessings of liberty to ourselves and our posterity, or
- Achieve a more perfect union.

If they cannot link their policies to one or more items on the list promoted by the Framers in the Preamble, then we should question whether those policies will help us at all.

For example, for decades now our government has used private prisons to house our ever-expanding prison population.[6] Our prison population is also mostly minorities, and many prisoners are being held for multiple years on nonviolent crimes. This long-term trend, in combination with the militarizing of city police forces, has exacerbated the "us versus them" feeling that exists among both minorities and the police. The excessive number of killings of black people by police in recent years, particularly without having to pay a penalty, resulted in the organization of the Black Lives Matter (BLM) movement. Members of the BLM movement contend that these policies deny justice to minorities, and their protests clearly indicate a break from domestic tranquility. They argue that they are not being provided a common defense from domestic enemies, that these policies are not promoting *their* general welfare, and they are not securing the blessings of liberty for them or their posterity. From their perspective, our Union is not more perfect under these conditions. These policies fail Black Americans and other minorities on every line of the checklist.

Yet, the 2020 election provides hope. Overall turnout set a record and turnout for minorities was also record setting. Black turnout in Georgia was most likely responsible for President Biden's win there. And, as dismal as the actions that caused the civil unrest of 2020 were (and how we have portrayed them in this work) there is hope that the message was heard by ordinary citizens and elected officials. Sure, some of them took away the wrong message, but we can hope that many more saw the merit in the case being made about injustice.

6 A small, but significant step was taken to correct this by the new administration of President Biden via an executive order banning future use by the Department of Justice of privately contracted prisons.

Final Thoughts

If nothing else, we have demonstrated, or perhaps just reiterated, that the words of the Preamble have meaning. They set the stage, they set the tone, they set the goals to be achieved by the document that follows them. Most important, perhaps, in that tone is the idea of a *more perfect* union, one that might never reach perfection but is ever striding toward it. The Preamble has taken something of a backseat to the more grandiose and directly impactful words found later in the Constitution, whether in the original document or in the amendments that followed.

This period of time of 2020 into early 2021 will, no doubt, be a period that we look back upon and realize that just as with the build-up to, and fighting of, the Civil War, the Great Depression, the unrest of protests against the Vietnam War, and the unrest of the Civil Rights movement, this was a time when our perfectibility was tested. What is it that the protesters of 2020 were fighting for, if not justice, eventual domestic tranquility, a common defense, the general welfare, and the blessings of liberty?

As the calendar flipped from 2020 to 2021, we fell off the path to perfection. We certainly did not insure domestic tranquility. The new year followed the questioning of our democratic process and the outcome of an election by the losing candidate for president, and brought a reaction, likely incited by that president's words, that threatened the very foundation of a more perfect union. Insurrectionists, bent on using violence, seeking to lynch the sitting Vice President and kill the speaker of the House, stormed the Capitol and delayed the congressional certification of the Electoral College vote. Five people died that day or soon after as a result of injuries sustained in the mayhem. A Capitol Police Officer died from natural causes after being attacked in the melee,[7] others committed suicide in the days and weeks that followed, and other civilians were trampled by their fellow rioters.[8] Yet, just two weeks later, on the very steps to the Capitol, the march of perfectibility began anew with

7 Reports indicate that he was attacked by "protestors" using bear spray.

8 Ironically, one Capitol Police officer's testimony from that day indicates that he was beaten with a Blue Lives Matter flag.

the inauguration of President Biden and inspired by the words of a 22-year-old poet, Amanda Gorman. Addressing the very point of striving for perfection Gorman wrote:

> And yes we are far from polished.
> Far from pristine.
> But that doesn't mean we are
> striving to form a union that is perfect.
> We are striving to forge a union with purpose,
> to compose a country committed to all cultures, colors, characters and
> conditions of man. (Gorman, January 20, 2021)

And, in a direct reference to what had taken place just two weeks earlier, right where she stood:

> A country that is bruised but whole,
> benevolent but bold,
> fierce and free.
> We will not be turned around
> or interrupted by intimidation,
> because we know our inaction and inertia
> will be the inheritance of the next generation.
> Our blunders become their burdens.
> But one thing is certain,
> If we merge mercy with might,
> and might with right,
> then love becomes our legacy,
> and change our children's birthright. (Gorman, January 20, 2021)

We have blundered, we have been subject to intimidation, we lack polish, and our Union is *far* from perfect. We are, as Madison noted, not angels, so government is necessary. We can look instead to Lincoln's appeal to our better angels. In the end, the words of the Preamble are not really separate goals, but the very essence of a more perfect union.

Bibliography

Dean, Howard. 2004. *You Have the Power: How to Take Back Our Country and Restore Democracy in America*. New York: Simon and Schuster.

Gorman, Amanda. 2021. January 20. "The Hill We Climb." Poem read at the Inauguration of President Joseph R. Biden.

Star Trek – The Omega Glory. Season 2, episode 23. Original air date March 1, 1968. Transcript at Chakoteya.net. Accessed February 27, 2021, http://www.chakoteya.net/StarTrek/54.htm.

Index

www.ingramcontent.com/pod-product-compliance
Ingram Content Group UK Ltd.
Pitfield, Milton Keynes, MK11 3LW, UK
UKHW021828100926
8556IPUK00003B/215

9 781433 188039